Thomas Woodhouse Levin

Six Lectures Introductory to the Philosophical Writings of Cicero

Thomas Woodhouse Levin

Six Lectures Introductory to the Philosophical Writings of Cicero

ISBN/EAN: 9783337069186

Printed in Europe, USA, Canada, Australia, Japan

Cover: Foto ©Thomas Meinert / pixelio.de

More available books at **www.hansebooks.com**

SIX LECTURES

INTRODUCTORY TO

THE PHILOSOPHICAL WRITINGS OF CICERO,

WITH

SOME EXPLANATORY NOTES ON THE SUBJECT-MATTER
OF THE ACADEMICA AND DE FINIBUS.

BY

T. W. LEVIN, M.A.

ST CATHARINE'S COLLEGE;
INTER-COLLEGIATE LECTURER ON LOGIC AND MORAL PHILOSOPHY.

"Facile etiam absentibus nobis veritas se ipsa defendet."

CAMBRIDGE:
DEIGHTON, BELL, AND CO.
LONDON: BELL AND DALDY.
1871.

WITH THE HOPE THAT

THE FOLLOWING LECTURES

MAY TO SOME SLIGHT EXTENT

AID IN REVIVING AN INTEREST IN SPECULATIVE SUBJECTS

AMONG THE STUDENTS OF THIS UNIVERSITY,

THE AUTHOR,

BY PERMISSION,

RESPECTFULLY INSCRIBES THEM

TO THE

REV. W. H. THOMPSON, D.D.

MASTER OF TRINITY COLLEGE, CAMBRIDGE,
AND LATE REGIUS PROFESSOR OF GREEK.

CAMBRIDGE,
October, 1871.

LECTURE I.

INTRODUCTORY.

"Non enim hominum interitu sententiæ quoque occidunt: sed lucem auctoris fortasse desiderant."

§ *a*. THE general object of these Lectures is to familiarize you with the distinctive spirit which pervades and informs the later manifestations of Greek speculative opinion. The character we shall there find exhibited was undoubtedly impressed by Pyrrho the Eliensic philosopher, diffused by the writings of Timon the Phliasian, and adopted by the representative men of the later Academy. Yet, influential as the teaching of Pyrrho was, the real nature and tendency of his doctrines have been strangely overlooked or misunderstood by most writers. To his figure has never yet been assigned its proper niche in the gallery of history. We shall therefore endeavour, if possible, to remedy this lack of just appreciation by making the aims and effects of Pyrrhonism one of the chief subjects of our enquiry. Another point we shall also consider is, the real extent to which the special doctrines of Pyrrho were entertained by the leaders of the so-called New Academy. This has always been a vexed question with historians, and one indeed which there is not much prospect of satisfactorily determining. Further, we shall attempt to present to you in as clear a light as possible, that problem which formed the centre of discussion between the Stoics and Academicians, and which is equally conspicuous in modern Metaphysics, namely, the nature and reality of the phenomena of perception. Some previous acquaintance with these subjects will, I hope, give the philosophical writings of Cicero a higher degree of interest for you than they have perchance hitherto possessed, since it is somewhat difficult for those not habituated to the atmosphere in which Cicero's characters think and speak, to follow their arguments or understand their allusions.

It is our purpose then to examine a portion of the history of Greek Philosophy comprised within the last three centuries before the commencement of the Christian era[1]. This is a period which perhaps has not commanded either the attention of historians[2], or the interest of students to the same degree as the age preceding, when Greek thought attained its highest development in the hands of Plato and

---

[1] We may consider the period before us to have commenced with Pyrrho, and closed with Cicero. The exact date of Pyrrho is uncertain, but he is known to have accompanied Alexander the Great on his Indian campaign. (Diogenes Laertius, IX. 61. 58.)

[2] Professor Maurice calls this period, "the lees of Greek philosophy," and favours it accordingly with a very brief notice. *Moral and Metaphysical Philosophy*, Part I. chap. VI. Liv. IV. sec. IV. Degerando remarks on the slight interest historians have taken in this part of Greek philosophy: "On est surpris de voir que la nouvelle Académie n'ait pas obtenu en général des historiens toute l'attention qu'elle meritait. Brucker, qui a consacré un livre entier à la philosophie Antédiluvienne, et de longs chapitres à des philosophes sans importance, accorde à peine quelques lignes à Philon et à Antiochus, quelque pages à Arcésilas et à Carnéade. On peut cependant consulter avec fruit *l'Academique* de Pierre de Valentia. Foucher: *Histoire des Académiciens* (Paris, 1690). *De philosophiâ Academicâ* (Paris, 1792). On trouve dans les *Mémoires de l'Académie Royale de Berlin en* 1748, une dissertation sur Clitomache, et dans ceux de l'Académie des Inscriptions la dissertation de

Aristotle; or as that succeeding, when the once brilliant flame of Athenian speculation flickered with the uncertain light of Alexandrian mysticism, before its final extinction in the obscurity of the dark ages. A careful consideration of the course of Greek thought during this period, may, I think, reveal to us many points of interest, which will render it worthy of minute investigation,—which may discover for it a character of its own, too marked to be overlooked by the historian of the development of human opinion,—and may show that it involves issues too important to be neglected by the critic of later systems of philosophy. Every event in general history should be viewed in connection with the circumstances which preceded and caused it, with those which accompanied and determined it, and with those which followed and resulted from it. So, in recording the successive phases of human opinion, which are the events in a history of philosophy, we must consider them with reference to preceding speculations, to those contemporaneous with them,

---

Gautier de Sibert." *Histoire comparée des Systèmes de Philosophie,*" Tome III. p. 110 (note). To these works of the Academy we may add the following, which profess to treat directly of the Pyrrhonian philosophy: *Dissert. de Philosophia Pyrrhonia* (Jac. Arrhenii, Upsal, 1708); *Dissert. de notione ac indole scepticismi, nominatim Pyrrhonismi* (Jo. Gottl. Munch, Altdorf, 1796); *Dissert. de Epoche Pyrrhonis* (God. Ploucquet, Tübingen, 1758); *Diss. Adumbratio quaestionis: an Pyrrhonis doctrina omnis tollatur virtus* (Ch. Vit. Kindervater, Leipzig, 1789); *Examen du Pyrrhonisme* (M. Crousaz). This book is, however, more a consideration of the results than the principles of Pyrrhonism, and is in fact little more than an attack on M. Bayle. Bishop Huet's *Traité philosophique de la faiblesse de l'esprit humain* is a good introduction to the subject, although it is encumbered with the false notion of perception through representative images prevalent among philosophers up to the age of Reid. Perhaps the fundamental problems of early scepticism are most clearly stated by Herbart, *Einleitung in die Philosophie*, 59. 173. Sextus Empiricus, who lived about the middle of the 3rd century A.D., wrote a voluminous treatise on the doctrines of Pyrrho and the Sceptics generally. The best edition is the Fabrician. Histories of Greek Philosophy by Brandis, Zeller, Schwegler and Lewes, are most accessible to English students.

and to those of succeeding generations. Hence, adopting this method of procedure in the discussion before us, we shall *first* give a preliminary sketch introducing the principal questions which occupied the attention of the schools of philosophers, the investigation of whose opinions is the object of the present course of Lectures.

Next, we shall as far as possible from original sources give the substance of these opinions with their bearing on contemporary schools of thought, and *finally*, we shall endeavour by criticism and comparison to determine the value their decisions or speculations may have for the present generation of labourers in similar fields of enquiry.

§ β. It is universally admitted that the great impulse Greek philosophy received from the teaching of Socrates was mainly owing to the *method* he introduced into the processes of speculation, and the ethical direction he gave to its aims. Before his advent, sages had thought and sceptics had doubted, but their thoughts had been as the wonder of infancy, the stirrings of that love of knowledge which Aristotle says is "a primary instinct of humanity;" for to them the great questions concerning man and the universe had first appeared in all their importance and mystery. "Indagatio ipsa rerum tum maximarum, tum etiam occultissimarum, habet oblectationem. Si vero aliquid occurret, quod verisimile videatur, humanissima completur animus voluptate[1]." The endeavour to discover the ultimate genesis of phenomena had already engaged the attention of the Ionian philosophers; the inability to reconcile the manifestations of these phenomena with the testimony of reason had given rise to the abstract idealism of the Eleatics;—the exclusive materialism of the *former* had resulted in the gloomy nihilism of Heraclitus,—and the subtle dialectic of the

[1] Lucullus, 41.

latter in the flippant scepticism of the Sophists[1]. But although the spontaneous activity of the human intellect had marked out distinct paths of speculation, the pre-Socratic age was distinguished by no definite method of conducting philosophical enquiries. Moreover, there was wanting some motive principle which might sustain the speculative faculties in investigations not directly connected with the common requirements of life. Thus philosophy soon came to be considered mere otiose and barren speculation; and, falling as an instrument of power and venality into the hands of the Sophists, it was not surprising that its professors suffered under the disrepute Plato describes in the Sixth Book of the Republic[2], and that the pursuit itself should be threatened with extinction.

At this crisis in the development of Greek thought, the genius of Socrates came to the aid of philosophy, and vindicated the higher energies of the human intellect by directing them into a worthy channel. Perceiving the barrenness and inutility of physical investigations, consisting as they did among the early thinkers in vain efforts to discover the causes and essences of things, he pronounced these ætiological and ontological speculations beyond the range of the human faculties, and taught that of all the objects of which man was conscious in the universe, he (man) himself was the most important subject of investigation (γνῶθι σεαυτόν).

[1] Gorgias Leontinus, sometime an adherent of the Eleatic school, was the author of a systematic treatise on scepticism thus described by Sextus Empiricus, "ἐν γὰρ τῷ ἐπιγραφομένῳ περὶ τοῦ μὴ ὄντος ἢ περὶ φύσεως τρία κατὰ τὸ ἑξῆς κεφάλαια κατασκευάζει, ἓν μὲν καὶ πρῶτον ὅτι οὐδέν ἐστι, δεύτερον ὅτι εἰ καὶ ἔστιν, ἀκατάληπτον ἀνθρώπῳ, τρίτον ὅτι εἰ καὶ καταληπτόν, ἀλλά τοί γε ἀνέξοιστον καὶ ἀνερμήνευτον τῷ πέλας."—*Adv. Math.* VII. 65.

[2] "Πρῶτον μὲν τοίνυν ἐκεῖνον τὸν θαυμάζοντα, ὅτι οἱ φιλόσοφοι οὐ τιμῶνται ἐν ταῖς πόλεσι, δίδασκέ τε τὴν εἰκόνα καὶ πειρῶ πείθειν, ὅτι πολὺ ἂν θαυμαστότερον ἦν, εἰ ἐτιμῶντο. 'Αλλὰ διδάξω, ἔφη. Καὶ ὅτι τοίνυν τἀληθῆ λέγεις, ὡς ἄχρηστοι τοῖς πολλοῖς οἱ ἐπιεικέστατοι τῶν ἐν φιλοσοφίᾳ." κ.τ.λ.—*Rep.* VI. 489.

The distinguishing feature then of all the philosophical enquiries which engaged the attention of the various schools founded by the followers of Socrates, was the endeavour to determine the relation and proper position of man with respect to the other objects in nature—man as a creature susceptible of pleasure and pain, perpetually aroused by his connection with these objects, and endowed with a primary and irresistible instinct to obtain for himself that fulfilment of his susceptibilities which he denominates happiness. The nature of happiness, the possibility of its attainment, and the means to be employed for this end, we find were the foremost questions of discussion, and the bases of the leading systems of thought during the four centuries which immediately preceded the Christian era; constituting a common groundwork sufficient for the perpetual antagonism of schools whose different solutions of the same problems were as opposed as those of the Cyrenaics, Stoics, and Pyrrhonists. "Nam omnis ratio vitæ definitione summi boni continetur: de qua qui dissident, de omni ratione vitæ dissident[1]." But although ethic was substituted for physic, as the object of intellectual activity we soon find that the very nature[2] of the questions constituting this science involved the necessity of more or less consideration of many of those branches of investigation which had occupied the main place in the field of thought during the predominance of the so-called physical subjects of speculation. Socrates had already attempted

---

[1] Lucullus, 43.
[2] "Die Tugendlehre aber bedarf der Kenntniss des Menschen; und sie wird um desto umher praktisch anwendbar, je mehr sio theils von der Erfahrung, theils von theoretischer Einsicht in die Natur des Menschen dasjenige in sich aufnimmt, was über die Veränderlichkeit des Menschen zum bessern und zum schlechtern Aufschluss giebt. Daher ihre Abhangigkeit von der Psychologie, und mittelbar von der Metaphysik."—Herbart's *Einleitung in die Philosophie*, Seite 157.

to solve the great problem of happiness by identifying it with virtue, and virtue again he defined to be synonymous with knowledge. Man according to his doctrine would, if he were acquainted with the true science of life, i.e. if he foresaw distinctly the real consequences[1] of his actions, or the real effects of the causes perpetually influencing him, necessarily only involve himself in the circumstances calculated to bring him the satisfaction of those desires implanted by nature. Hence, the true meaning of the maxim of Socrates—"κακὸς ἑκὼν οὐδείς"—no man *would* be willingly evil because no man *could* be willingly unhappy—vice was the result of ignorance, as knowledge inevitably led to virtue—knowledge then was indispensable to a right practice of virtue, and virtue constituted the true happiness of man. We shall see that this notion of Socrates, viz. that evil was the result of intellectual not moral depravity, had a most powerful influence upon the subsequent development of Greek thought, and in fact forms the leading distinction between Christian and heathen ethical philosophy. Socrates imagined that by appealing to the universal and irresistible instinct of humanity towards happiness, he would establish a permanent motive for the practice of virtue, and the pursuit of knowledge. No sooner, however, were his doctrines put to the test than the futility of this expectation was abundantly demonstrated.

§ γ. On the one hand, it was maintained by the sensualists, or Hedonistic sect of moralists, that if, as seemed to be universally admitted, human knowledge was purely relative and subjective—if, according to the apophthegm of Protagoras, "man was the measure of all things," then our sensations were the only objects of which we had absolute know-

[1] "Δοκεῖ δὲ καὶ ἡ ἐμπειρία ἡ περὶ ἕκαστα ἀνδρεία τις εἶναι· ὅθεν καὶ ὁ Σωκράτης ᾠήθη ἐπιστήμην εἶναι τὴν ἀνδρείαν." Aristotle, *Eth. Nicom.* III. 11. 6.

ledge, and of which we could predicate certain existence (τά τε πάθη, καταληπτά. Ἔλεγον οὖν αὐτὰ, οὐκ ἀφ' ὧν γίνεται)[1]. Pleasure and pain[2], consequently, were the only criteria of good and evil. The natural tendency of man to obtain the one and avoid the other, had been expressed by the institution of conventional canons of right and wrong. Justice was law, some said the law of the strongest, others the instinctive means of defence adopted by the weak; and similarly with regard to the other virtues, they had no existence beyond that obtained from the sanction of law, tradition, or custom. A good man therefore practised virtue in order to avoid censure or punishment. (Μηδέν τε εἶναι φύσει δίκαιον, ἢ καλὸν, ἢ αἰσχρόν· ἀλλὰ νόμῳ καὶ ἔθει. Ὁ μέντοι σπουδαῖος οὐδὲν ἄτοπον πράξει διὰ τὰς ἐπικειμένας ζημίας καὶ δόξας[3].) Here then was one result from the Socratic theory that virtue, knowledge and happiness were co-ordinate with each other. On the other hand, there was another sect among the disciples of Socrates headed by Antisthenes and Diogenes, who, starting from the same subjective idea of pleasure and pain, but instituting a more subtle analysis of the relation of those feelings to their causes, arrived at very opposite conclusions with respect to the attainment of happiness. They perceived that pleasure was the equilibrium between the desires or affections of the human mind and the means provided by nature for their gratification, and that experience continually showed the inadequacy of the latter to meet the demands of the former. Consequently, said they, it is impossible, according to the present constitution of

[1] Diogenes Laertius, Lib. II. cap. VIII. 92.
[2] "Δοκεῖ δ' αὐτοῖς καὶ τέλος εὐδαιμονίας διαφέρειν. Τέλος μὲν γὰρ εἶναι τὴν κατὰ μέρος ἡδονήν· εὐδαιμονίαν δὲ, τὸ ἐκ τῶν μερικῶν ἡδονῶν σύστημα, αἷς συναριθμοῦνται καὶ αἱ παρῳχηκυῖαι, καὶ αἱ μέλλουσαι. Εἶναί τε τὴν μερικὴν ἡδονὴν, δι' αὐτὴν αἱρετήν· τὴν δ' εὐδαιμονίαν, οὐ δι' αὐτήν, ἀλλὰ διὰ τὰς κατὰ μέρος ἡδονάς."—Diogenes Laertius, Lib. II. cap. VIII. 87, 88.
[3] Diogenes Laertius, Lib. II. cap. VIII. 93.

things, to expect satisfaction from the action of external causes. The only alternative was to moderate the cravings of humanity as much as possible in order to meet the paucity of means at hand for their fulfilment. Thus the Cynics hoped to live in proud independence of the circumstances around them, superior to pain, unallured by pleasure; and, as if to form the most marked antithesis possible to the followers of Aristippus, they, as Diogenes Laertius tells us, used to maintain that they owed no allegiance to any laws but those of virtue. (Καὶ τὸν σοφὸν οὐ κατὰ τοὺς κειμένους νόμους πολιτεύεσθαι, ἀλλὰ κατὰ τὸν τῆς ἀρετῆς[1].) The sentiments of both schools on this point were the natural corollaries from their respective systems. The Eudaimonists, finding the end of life in pleasure, were compelled to consider the individual as dependent, social, and interested in the welfare of the community of which he was a member. His canon of right and wrong, therefore, would be the laws to which society had agreed to submit; whereas the Cynic, isolated and self-sufficient, was unwilling to confess himself amenable to any claims but those of what he considered his own higher nature. The one affirmed there was no *virtue* but that constituted by *law*, the other that there was no *law* but that constituted by *virtue*. It was perhaps in view of these conflicting conclusions respecting that which was the common object of both parties, viz. the attainment of happiness, that Pyrrho, the Eliensic philosopher, was induced to attempt on his own part the institution of an art of life. He probably compared the systems of the Cynics and Cyrenaics with the views of Socrates himself, a knowledge of whose opinions it is said was imparted to him by his fellow-townsman Phædo[2],

---

[1] Diogenes Laertius, Lib. VI. cap. I. v. 11.

[2] "Auch darf uns die Frage, auf welchem Wege er Kenntniss vom Sokrates erlangen konnte, gar nicht in Verlegenheit setzen, wenn auch weder Dryson noch Klinomachus, chronologischer Schwierigkeiten wegen, seine

and the result of this comparison must have been soon to reveal to him that neither of these sects of philosophers had developed the Socratic notion of happiness in a way that would have been endorsed by Socrates himself. Some authors have striven to point out traces of the Socratic doctrines in the teaching of Pyrrho, and we find Cicero refers to his school as one of those professing to be sprung from the Athenian sage (fuerunt etiam alia genera philosophorum, qui se omnes fere Socraticos esse dicebant; Eretriacorum, Herilliorum, Megaricorum, Pyrrhoniorum[1].) It seems to us, however, that the Socratic influence is only so far discernible in the Pyrrhonian system as determining the subject about which it treated, viz. human happiness. But, as we have before observed, this question was the fundamental problem of all the post-Socratic schools of philosophy. Mr Grote remarks[2] upon this point: "Tennemann seeks to make out considerable analogy between Socrates and Pyrrho. But it seems to me that the analogy only goes thus far—that both agreed in repudiating all speculations not ethical. But in regard to Ethics, the two differed materially. Socrates maintained that Ethics were matter of science, and the proper subject of study. Pyrrho, on the other hand, seems to have thought that speculation was just as useless, and science just as unattainable, upon Ethics, as upon Physics; that nothing was to be attended to except feelings, and nothing cultivated except good dispositions." Cannot there, then, be a science of feelings; and was it not exactly this which constituted the positive side of the Pyrrhonian system? In truth Pyrrho, as he is represented to us by ancient

---

Lehrer waren, da Phädo aus derselben Stadt war, und daselbst auch eine Schule errichtet hatte."—Tennemann's *Geschichte der Philosophie*, zweiter Band, Seite 171.

[1] *De Oratore*, III. 17.
[2] *History of Greece*, Vol. VIII. note, p. 665.

writers, appears in two different, and by some thought incompatible characters, viz. Pyrrho the moralist, and Pyrrho the sceptic. By Cicero he is mentioned solely in the former light, as making virtue the single aim and object of his teaching. (Pyrrho—qui virtute constituta, nihil omnino, quod appetendum sit, relinquat[1].) And it is a singular fact that this author never once mentions Pyrrho in connection with the sceptical philosophy, not even in those fragments of his works which are especially devoted to the discussion of this subject[2]. Sextus Empiricus, on the other hand, to whose voluminous treatise we are mainly indebted for the information we possess concerning the spirit and tendency of the Pyrrhonian philosophy, emphatically proclaims Pyrrho as the author of the sceptical method, and he is by most modern writers recognised[3], and certainly popularly known, as the father of scepticism. The question then arises, how far these two characters are reconcilable as belonging to the same individual; and we have endeavoured in the ensuing chapter to show that in the blending of these apparently discordant elements lies the whole originality of early Pyrrhonism. Scepticism was adopted by Pyrrho as an instrument for the attainment of virtue, and the only means of securing the greatest amount of happiness. Let us for a moment consider what may have been the steps by which he arrived at this conviction.

§ 5. It is often not difficult among the circumstances or conditions of life to which a great thinker has been subject, to detect some cause or other which had probably a determining influence upon the direction of his speculations. If Antisthenes had been as wealthy as Aristip-

[1] *De Finibus*, IV. 16.
[2] *Prior and post Academics*.
[3] Cudworth's *Treatise on Eternal and Immutable Morality*, chap. 1, 2. 527.

pus, or Aristippus as poor as Antisthenes, would they ever have been celebrated as the respective founders of the Cynic and Cyrenaic sects of philosophers? Little is known of the life of Pyrrho, and that little is not calculated to throw much light upon the formation of his opinions. There is, however, one circumstance connected with him which we think may have been somewhat conducive to the development of his peculiar views—we mean his profession, that of an artist. Pyrrho we know derived his disbelief in all science from the uncertain character of sensible perception, and, as we shall find in the δέκα τρόποι, many of his arguments found upon the illusive nature of judgments concerning the magnitude and figure of external objects[1]. It is not improbable then that the attention of Pyrrho was especially directed to this subject by the frequent opportunity he had of observing in the practice of his art the various artificial effects that could be produced by a knowledge of the laws of perspective. Again, as a moralist, in the work of Sextus Empiricus there is nothing stated with such emphatic distinctness as the decided and uncompromising hostility which Pyrrhon-

---

[1] Even those who are least favorable to the Pyrrhonist doctrines admit that there is some force in their arguments based upon the discrepancy of visible perception. "On peut bien savoir par les sens qu'un tel corps est plus grand qu'un autre corps; mais on ne saurait savoir avec certitude quelle est la grandeur véritable et naturelle de chaque corps; et, pour comprendre cela, il n'y a qu'à considérer que si tout le monde n'avait jamais regardé les objets extérieurs qu'avec des lunettes qui les grossissent, il est certain qu'on ne se serait figuré les corps et toutes les mesures des corps, que selon la grandeur dans laquelle ils nous auraient été représentés par ces lunettes: or, nos yeux mêmes sont des lunettes, et nous ne savons pas précisément s'ils ne diminuent point ou n'augmentent point les objets que nous voyons, et si les lunettes artificielles que nous croyons les diminuer ou les augmenter, ne les établissent point, au contraire, dans leur grandeur véritable; et partant, on ne connaît pas certainement la grandeur absolue et naturelle de chaque corps."—Arnauld, *La Logique de Port-Royal*, p. 281.

ism bore to the voluptuous philosophy of the Cyrenaics[1]. May it not have been that this determined opposition to the idea of pleasure containing the essentials of happiness was in some part due to the observations he had made of the disastrous effects which attended its pursuit? for it was his art to depict the human countenance distorted by ungovernable passions. In truth, if man could have been brought to view life with the apathy Pyrrho so assiduously endeavoured to inculcate, there would have been few objects left for the employment of the limner's talent. To the writings of Democritus and Homer, which we are told were the favourite works of Pyrrho, we may undoubtedly attribute many of his speculative and moral conclusions.

Democritus is said to have been the first of the materialist philosophers who, contrary to the natural beliefs of mankind, distinguished in the sensible qualities of things those which were real, permanent and objective, from those which were only apparent and relative, thus furnishing a plausible pretext for the paradoxes of the early Sceptics. The perusal of the Homeric poems describing the conflicts of cities and nations, had probably the same effect on the mind of Pyrrho as the study of the history of individuals revealed by the expression stamped upon their features. Reflecting on the strife and misery consequent on the indulgence of love, anger and ambition,

"Hunc amor, ira quidem communiter urit utrumque.
Quidquid delirant reges plectuntur Achivi,
Seditione, dolis, scelere atque libidine et ira
Iliacos intra muros peccatur et extra[2]."

[1] "διαφέρει δὲ αὐτῆς· ἐπειδὴ ἐκείνη μὲν τὴν ἡδονὴν καὶ τὴν λείαν τῆς σαρκὸς κίνησιν τέλος εἶναι λέγει, ἡμεῖς δὲ τὴν ἀταραξίαν, ᾗ ἐναντιοῦται τὸ κατ' ἐκείνους τέλος· καὶ γὰρ παρούσης τῆς ἡδονῆς καὶ μὴ παρούσης, ταραχὰς ὑπομένει ὁ διαβεβαιούμενος τέλος εἶναι τὴν ἡδονήν."—*Hyp.* I. 31. 215.

[2] Horatii *Epistolarum*, I. 2. 13—16.

he would naturally be led to the conviction that of all the paths to happiness, the one making pleasure its sole end and aim was the least likely to lead to the expected goal, and that the truly wise and truly happy were alone

> "those who far aloof
> From envy, hate and pity, spite and scorn,
> Live the great life which all our greatest fain
> Would follow, center'd in eternal calm."

Some historians refer the sceptical and moral elements in the views of Pyrrho to the teaching of Bryson, son of Stilpo, the Megaric philosopher, but this hypothesis must be rejected on account of chronological difficulties. Others again have conjectured that Pyrrho derived many of his doctrines from the Gymnosophists, with whose institutions he is said to have become acquainted when he was in India with the expedition of Alexander. There is certainly a strong Oriental tinge in the idea of $\dot{a}\tau a\rho a\xi \acute{\iota}a$, or tranquillity, inculcated by Pyrrho as the *summum bonum* of existence. But as this notion was prominent in the system of the Cynics, and afterwards in that of the Stoics, there was no reason for supposing Pyrrho should have been indebted for it to foreign influences. Indeed the tendency to fatalism, which is the groundwork of all the apathetic schools of Greece, is essentially characteristic of Aryan thought. We do not, however, for this reason consider Greek philosophy any more than Greek language was directly derivative from eastern sources. As the many analogies between the forms of the Sanscrit and Greek languages only betray that both were originally from a common stock, so the parallelism of thought discernible in the Greek and Indian philosophies is an evidence certainly of consanguinity, but not necessarily of filiation. Those who read the treatise of Cicero on the subject of 'whether virtue be sufficient for a happy life,' will find there suggested a train of reflection similar to that which must have led Pyrrho to the adoption of his solution of the question. After having peremptorily dismissed the idea of pleasure as conducive to happiness, we may imagine his meditations to have concluded thus : "Quod si est, qui vim fortunæ, qui omnia humana, quæ cuique accidere possunt, tolerabilia ducat, ex quo nec timor eum, nec angor attingat: idemque, si nihil concupiscat nulla efferatur animi inani voluptate, quid est, cur is non beatus sit: et si hæc virtute efficiuntur quid est, cur virtus ipsa per se non efficiat beatos[1]?" At this point the difficulty would have presented itself which must inevitably occur to any one possessing the slightest experience of human nature: How is it possible that the suppression of natural impulses can, at least in the process, be attended with happiness?—the very notion is self-contradictory. How can peace and tranquillity be present where there is a continual struggle? Virtue, if it must be practised at the cost of a perpetual conflict with nature, would be a harder taskmaster even than pleasure. Here then Pyrrho seems to have thought he had discovered a method of reconciling the claims of our higher and lower nature. If the denial of desires was too painful to be consistent with the idea of happiness, were there no means, *not* of *extinguishing* the tumultuous cravings of nature, *but* of *preventing* them from *ever arising?* This object Pyrrho thought might be accomplished by the cultivation of a habit of doubt, namely, whether those qualities in objects a belief in the existence of which is the parent of desire, had any absolute, necessary, or permanent power.

Such was the moral aim of the Pyrrhonian scepticism, which we will not discuss further at present, having made it the subject of the following lecture.

[1] *Tusc. Disput.* v. 6.

Before concluding these introductory remarks, however, on the doctrines of Pyrrho, we must advert to some difficulties meeting us in the historical development of our subject.

§ ε. In treating of the doctrines and influence of Pyrrho and the Pyrrhonists it is not easy to determine, from the historical remains extant, which are the views of Pyrrho himself—which are due to the promulgators of his opinions—and, above all, which are the individual conclusions of Sextus Empiricus his expounder. In comparing, therefore, the tenets of the Pyrrhonists with those of the New Academicians, the question arises: How much of the accounts delivered to us by Sextus Empiricus are we to regard as essentially typical of Pyrrhonism? Pyrrho himself left no writings, but his friend and pupil Timon of Phlius compiled his celebrated satirical poem (the Silli) with the object of enunciating the principles and aims of scepticism[1]. This work, however, is unfortunately lost, but from the few fragments we find of it quoted by other authors we can gather what were the distinguishing characteristics of early Pyrrhonism. From these we infer that the intention of Pyrrho was mainly that which we have already indicated, viz. to construct an art of life on a basis of doubt[2] ($\dot{a}\pi o\rho i a$) —doubt was to lead to suspension of judgment ($\dot{\epsilon}\pi o\chi\dot{\eta}$), and this again to tranquillity of mind ($\dot{a}\tau a\rho a\xi i a$). Through the equilibrium of reasons ($i\sigma o\sigma\theta\dot{\epsilon}\nu\epsilon\iota a$) was engendered an equilibrium of motives, and hence an absence of emotion and action. This form of Pyrrhonism, like most of the tentative systems of philosophy which sprang up on the death of Socrates, did not survive the introduction of the more scientifically conceived schools of thought consequent upon the promulgation of the Aristotelian method. The sceptical portion of Pyrrhonism was then adopted by Arcesilaus, and

---

[1] Diogenes Laertius, Lib. IX. cap. XI. 5.
[2] *Præparat. Evang.* XIV. 18 (758 A.). Ὁ δέ γε μαθητὴς αὐτοῦ Τίμων φησὶ, δεῖν τὸν μέλλοντα εὐδαιμονήσειν, κ.τ.λ.

employed mainly, we think, as a weapon against the Stoical dogmatists by him, and afterwards by Carneades and the New Academicians. When the conflict between this latter sect and the Stoics had been terminated by the desertion of Antiochus to the Porch (or rather by the introduction of Stoical opinions into the Academy), Pyrrhonism is said to have been revived by Ænesidemus and Agrippa. We do not think, however, that this second school of Pyrrhonism had much in common with the first, but was only a prolongation of the Academic scepticism. That there was a difference, we admit, between the scepticism of Ænesidemus, Agrippa, Menodotus, and that of the New Academy, but the distinction was this: Carneades only opposed his scepticism to the dogmatic pretensions of the Stoics, reserving at the same time the traditions of the older Academy concerning the possibility of *à priori* knowledge; whereas the Empirical sceptics whom Sextus Empiricus still denominated Pyrrhonists were absolute sceptics, because in denying the certainty of empirical knowledge they denied virtually the possibility of knowledge altogether. Carneades and the New Academicians carried their scepticism as a shield, the Pyrrhonists wore it as a garment. Yet we think there was less difference between the New Academy and the later Pyrrhonists than between the earlier and second school of Pyrrhonism. Sextus Empiricus distinctly repudiates Ænesidemus for mingling the dogmas of Heraclitus among the sceptical doctrines "οἱ περὶ τὸν Αἰνησίδημον ἔλεγον ὁδὸν εἶναι τὴν σκεπτικὴν ἀγωγὴν ἐπὶ τὴν Ἡρακλείτειον φιλοσοφίαν, διότι προηγεῖται τοῦ τἀναντία περὶ τὸ αὐτὸ ὑπάρχειν τὸ τἀναντία περὶ τὸ αὐτὸ φαίνεσθαι[1];" then, after distinguishing clearly between the Heraclitic and sceptical views, he adds: "ἄτοπον δέ ἐστιν τὸ τὴν μαχομένην ἀγωγὴν ὁδὸν εἶναι λέγειν τῆς αἱρέσεως ἐκείνης ᾗ μάχεται. ἄτοπον ἄρα τὸ τὴν σκεπτικὴν ἀγωγὴν ἐπὶ τὴν Ἡρα-

[1] *Hyp.* I. 29. 210.

κλείτειον φιλοσοφίαν ὁδὸν εἶναι λέγειν¹." Ænesidemus is, however, still more emphatically separated from the older Pyrrhonism by his abandonment of the original object of the whole system, viz., the attainment of ἀταραξία. Aristocles in Eusebius, quoting the words of Timon concerning the principles and aims of Pyrrho, says: "Τοῖς μέντοι διακειμένοις οὕτω περιέσεσθαι Τίμων φησὶ πρῶτον μὲν ἀφασίαν, ἔπειτα δ' ἀταραξίαν Αἰνησίδημος δὲ ἡδονήν²." Comparing this passage with the uncompromising disgust with which the idea of pleasure is viewed in the 1st book of the Hypotyposes, we should infer that Ænesidemus can scarcely be reckoned a follower of Pyrrho. Tennemann seems to think that the later Pyrrhonists are distinguished from the earlier principally by having shifted their sceptical point of view, the former professing mere subjective doubt, whereas the latter had extended this doubt to the nature of the object: "Die Zusammenstellung der Widersprüche in den Systemen der Dogmatiker musste zum Beweise das Unvermögens der Objekte dienen, ihre Natur zu erkennen zu geben, und hieraus folgerten sie die Unverlässigkeit der Sinne und des Verstandes zur Erkenntniss der Wahrheit. Die neuern Skeptiker, durch die Gegengründe der Dogmatiker veranlasst, welche den Skepticismus von der Seite vorzüglich angriffen, dass er selbst eine objective Behauptung enthalte, diese nämlich, die Objecte sind unvermögend, eine Erkenntniss zu begründen, gaben mit grösser Einsicht diese auf, und blieben bei der Ansicht stehen, dass bis jetzt in keinem Stücke etwas entschieden sey, und die widersprechenden Behauptungen den Verstand in eine Art von Gleichgewicht setzen, dass er weder bejahend noch verneinend zu entscheiden wagt³."

---

[1] *Hyp.* I. 29. 212.
[2] *Præpar. Evang.* Lib. XIV. 18. 758 B.
[3] Tennemann, *Geschichte der Philosophie.* Zweiter Band, s. 186.

The information we possess as to the real opinions of Carneades is not much more direct than that concerning those of Pyrrho: in both cases it is but the echo, not the voice of the master we hear; for Carneades, like Pyrrho, left no record of his own tenets. As Sextus Empiricus was the expounder of the Pyrrhonian method, so we may consider Cicero to have been the mouthpiece of Carneades, at least on the subject of metaphysics—on points of morality Cicero professes entire disagreement with the New Academy. We have, however, among the philosophical writings of Cicero, but one really undertaking to discuss expressly the views of the later Academy on speculative subjects. This treatise, intended to present an account of the course of the polemic between the New Academicians and the Stoics concerning the grounds of certitude of human knowledge, is one of the least satisfactory of the productions of this great author. No writer has ever better understood, or more distinctly stated, the requisites of a finished philosophical style, viz. to handle important points exhaustively, subordinate ones tersely (grandia ornate, enucleate minora dicere[1]); yet in the Lucullus this canon seems almost to have been reversed; fundamental principles are scarcely approached, while assertions instead of arguments on either side are repeated with tedious iteration. The inadequacy of the treatment indeed to the exigencies of the subject did not escape the attention of Cicero himself; and, as he explains to us the circumstances[2] which occasioned it, there

[1] *De Finibus*, IV. 3.
[2] "Illam ἀκαδημικὴν σύνταξιν totam ad Varronem traduximus. Primo fuit Catuli, Luculli, Hortensii: deinde, quia παρὰ τὸ πρέπον videbatur, quod erat hominibus nota, non illa quidem ἀπαιδευσία, sed in iis rebus ἀτριψία, simul ac veni ad villam, eosdem illos sermones ad Catonem Brutumque transtuli."—*Ep. ad Att.* XIII. 16. "Hæc Academica, ut scis, cum Catulo, Lucullo, Hortensio, contuleram. Sane in personas non cadebant. Erant enim λογικώτερα, quam ut illi de iis somniasse umquam viderentur."—*Ep.* 19. It would appear from these extracts that Cicero in his first edition adapted his method

is no place for criticism. In fact, he recalled the work in question, and substituted for it another dissertation on the same subject (*Acad. post*). Of this there are but twelve sections extant, the last of which only introduces Arcesilaus, and therefore just commences to expound the peculiar views of the New Academy.

§ ζ. The relation of the New to the Old Academy must be mainly determined by the degree of sincerity with which the sceptical or negative arm of philosophy was employed by the former. If we are to believe the testimony of Sextus Empiricus, Arcesilaus was a sceptic to his adversaries, but a maintainer of the more positive part of the Platonic doctrines to his friends. " φασὶν ὅτι κατὰ μὲν τὸ πρόχειρον Πυρρώνειος ἐφαίνετο εἶναι, κατὰ δὲ τὴν ἀλήθειαν δογματικὸς ἦν, καὶ ἐπεὶ τῶν ἑταίρων ἀπόπειραν ἐλάμβανε διὰ τῆς ἀπορηματικῆς, εἰ εὐφυῶς ἔχουσι πρὸς τὴν ἀνάληψιν τῶν Πλατωνικῶν δογμάτων, δόξαι αὐτὸν ἀπορητικὸν εἶναι, τοῖς μέντοι γε εὐφυέσι τῶν ἑταίρων τὰ Πλάτωνος παρεγχειρεῖν[1]." As we have already remarked, we think it probable that the integrity of Platonism was preserved by Carneades and Philo. How else can we interpret the position of the latter—that we could know things *per se*, but not through the cataleptic phantasm? (ὅσον μὲν ἐπὶ τῷ Στωϊκῷ κριτηρίῳ, τουτέστι τῇ καταληπτικῇ φαντασίᾳ, ἀκατάληπτα εἶναι τὰ πράγματα, ὅσον δὲ ἐπὶ τῇ φύσει τῶν πραγμάτων αὐτῶν κατάληπτα[2]). It seems to us indeed that the real cause of hostility between the Stoics and Academicians was this very adherence by the latter to the views of Plato, in opposition to the empirical and materialist philosophy

of treating the subject to the capacity of the assumed interlocutors; hence, the constant lack of logical sequence discernible in the Lucullus, and the repetition of puerile and frivolous matter. There is no doubt, however, that the amended work was as perfect as the other was deficient even from the meagre but invaluable fragment which has survived.

[1] *Hyp.* I. 33. 234.   [2] *Hyp.* I. 33. 235.

of the former. One of the first effects of the triumph of the Aristotelian philosophy had been to re-open the great question concerning the certainty of knowledge. Plato had proclaimed his ideal theory, as the only refuge from scepticism, the only foundation of absolute truth; therefore, on the overthrow of this theory, the opinions of the Sceptics touching the relativity and consequent uncertainty of all things had become more and more prevalent. It was to stem this torrent of scepticism that Zeno and the Stoics, while maintaining the empirical nature of all our knowledge, endeavoured to derive a basis of certitude from those intuitive perceptions of the real qualities of objects which they thought were to be found in the cataleptic phantasm. Thus the attention of philosophers was concentrated upon the psychological process, in which material objects of knowledge assumed the form of mental perceptions, and on the validity of the assent or instinctive belief ($\sigma\upsilon\gamma\kappa\alpha\tau\acute{\alpha}\theta\epsilon\sigma\iota\varsigma$) afforded by the mind to the testimony of consciousness. It was the opposition of the Academy to the Stoics on this point which constituted the scepticism of the former—a scepticism relative indeed only to the empiricism of the latter; and which, as we have seen, for this reason differed essentially from the scepticism of the Pyrrhonists. In this controversy, on the one hand, the question at issue was whether or not a realist theory of perception could be demonstrated to be true. That any theory of perception is *demonstrable*, especially by empiricism, involved a self-contradiction, because the facts of consciousness which were called as evidence could only be interpreted by the *assumption* of the theory, and yet upon these *facts alone* could any theory be based.

The New Academicians, on the other hand, still holding the ground formerly occupied by Plato that the mind in perception was conscious of nothing but its own modifications, the mere shadows of external objects, showed irrefutably that all hope of escaping from mere subjective knowledge was impossible (πάντα εἶναι ἀκατάληπτα); and so the contest continued, from Arcesilaus to Antiochus, without hope of any satisfactory termination. Each side, safe under the shelter of its own theory, eagerly watched for the weak place in that of its adversary—

> "ἧσσον δὲ λόγχαις· ἀλλ' ὑφίζανον κύκλοις,
> ὅπως σίδηρος ἐξολισθάνοι μάτην.
> εἰ δ' ὄμμ' ὑπερσχὸν ἴτυος ἅτερος μάθοι,
> λόγχην ἐνώμα στόματι, προφθῆναι θέλων [1]."—

and thus, without ever fairly grappling the problem, they left it as a legacy for later philosophers to attempt to solve.

It may be gathered from these preliminary remarks, that the main subject which is to occupy our attention in the following Lectures, must be the consideration of the features and tendencies of ancient scepticism; for it is obvious, scepticism in one form or another was the essential characteristic of each of the three schools—that of Pyrrho, of the New Academy, and of the later Pyrrhonists. We shall therefore conclude this introductory chapter with a few observations on this aspect of Greek philosophy.

§ η. Scepticism is one of those words which, from the earliest date of their use, seem to convey a meaning different from their real signification. According to the etymology of the word, a sceptic was simply *an enquirer*, and we have the name σκεπτική used always synonymously with ζητητική by Sextus Empiricus. But through that habit of confusing cause with effect we so often see indicated in the use of words, σκεπτική was soon understood to mean solely ἀπορητική, or the art of doubting. Although, however, the Sceptics

---

[1] *Phœnissæ*, line 1397.

professedly adhered to the literal meaning of the word as justly applied to themselves, few will hesitate to admit that the love of doubt is a more prominent feature throughout their system than the love of investigation.

M. Cousin, synthetically deducing all the schools of philosophy from à priori consideration of the instinctive tendencies inherent in the human mind, determines scepticism to be an inevitable result from the opposing dogmatisms of sensualism and idealism, "le sensualisme, l'idealisme, et le scepticisme." Such is the inevitable succession in the human mind,—a like order of succession then we must expect to find in the history of the development of human thought; and, according to the facts M. Cousin adduces, such seems to have been actually the case. But this theory is obviously only applicable to scepticism considered as a manifestation of the doubting, not the enquiring element in the mind. Every new system of thought must be sceptical in relation to the system it supplants, and the transition from one to the other necessarily supposes the exercise of that zetetic faculty which scepticism primarily implied. In this sense, therefore, scepticism would be the alternate link in the successive phases of opinion, the motive or dynamical element in the intellectual constitution of man continually urging him forward in his search after truth,—a search which, although the attainment of its object may be impossible, evokes the employment of his noblest powers. "Speculative truth (says Sir W. Hamilton) is subordinate to speculation itself, and its value is directly measured by the quantity of energy which it occasions[1]"—scepticism and true philosophy are thus identical.

The moment a philosopher begins to dogmatize, he ceases to be a philosopher, for then he virtually admits his search after truth is at an end. Of course the dogmatic and philo-

[1] Sir W. Hamilton's *Discussions* (II. Essay). "Philosophy of Perception," p. 40.

sophic tendencies in human nature *will* find expression: the former as the stable, conservative, practical; the latter as the moving, progressive, speculative.

The due adjustment then of these apparently conflicting elements will constitute a healthy intellectual tone either in the individual or in what is termed the spirit of the age, which is but the common expression of an aggregate of individuals; and the preponderance of the dogmatical or sceptical tendencies is always indicative of an abnormal state in any period of the history of human thought.

"The negative side of Grecian speculation stands quite as prominently marked, and occupies as large a measure of the intellectual force of their philosophers, as the positive side. It is not simply to arrive at a conclusion, sustained by a certain measure of plausible premise—and then to proclaim it as an authoritative dogma, silencing or disparaging all objectors—that Grecian speculation aspires. To unmask not only positive falsehood, but even affirmation without evidence, exaggerated confidence in what was only doubtful, and show of knowledge without the reality—to look at a problem on all sides, and set forth all the difficulties attending its solution—to take account of deductions from the affirmative evidence, even in the case of conclusions accepted as true upon the balance—all this will be found pervading the march of their greatest thinkers. As a condition of all progressive philosophy, it is not less essential that the grounds of negation should be freely exposed than the grounds of affirmation. We shall find the two going hand in hand, and the negative vein indeed the more impressive and characteristic of the two, from Zeno downwards in our history[1]." It seems evident that scepticism always has been, and always must be necessary to the advancement of human thought: the paradox of one age may become an axiom in the next, a prejudice in

---

[1] *History of Greece* (Grote), chap. XLVII. p. 472.

the succeeding; and if there was no disposition to question, examine, and sift the grounds of opinion, intellect would stagnate, and the natural aspirations of man onwards and upwards would be blunted and impeded. Why then has the word "scepticism" such an obnoxious sound to the ears of most people, that the very enquiry into its character and history is looked upon with mistrust? It is for this reason, *that*, in the infancy of thought among the Greeks, and to a great degree in modern times, the limits and functions of the different fields of activity of the human mind have never been properly or adequately defined. In Greece, philosophy, science and religion being alike treated as products of reason, the conclusions of one were considered applicable to the solution of problems properly belonging to the other two. Thus it was that the false methods of physical enquiry, which seemed to render the attainment of any positive science impossible, threw an unhealthy feeling of doubt and discouragement on speculative or philosophical pursuits, and subverted or clouded with uncertainty all the foundations of natural morality. When virtue and knowledge were considered identical, what wonder that to impugn the validity of the latter seemed to involve a questioning of the authority of the former. So in our own day the claims of philosophy, science and religion are held by many to be conflicting, and they who rely upon one are frequently led to discard the other. The man of science certain in his results, confident in his processes, despises the dreaming philosopher, who in his search after truth appears to neglect all that is substantial and practical; *both*, confident that the reason of man is potent to measure the mysteries of the universe, look upon faith, which is beyond the range of reason because it is above it, as the offspring of bigotry and superstition. In fact, however, the tendency of zetetic philosophy, which we think is all philosophy, is, as we shall endeavour in the following pages to show, to render man more and more dependent upon faith, faith being the principle on which the validity of all the processes of reason must ultimately depend. Every new phase of speculative opinion must lead the thoughtful observer to the conviction that it is not given to the human intellect to unlock the secrets of the absolute—man is not the measure of all things —"ἀτελὲς οὐδὲν οὐδενὸς μέτρον[1]." If philosophy has succeeded in convincing the proud reason of man of this fact, it surely has contributed something to the interests of religion—if it points out to science her proper domain and limit, science cannot but admit herself on this account under great obligations to speculation. It is then with these objects in view that the historian of ancient thought should engage in his task; not treating opinions as the venerable ruins of bygone ages, but as the expressions of tendencies in the human mind, which, being constant in their operation, must perpetually recur as long as human nature remains the same; so that any judgment passed will be of as much importance as a contribution to the study of modern as of ancient thought, and, by deciding for ever those questions the recurrence of which may be calculated on as isochronous perturbations, leave the attention of philosophers free to be concentrated on new fields of discovery and speculation.

[1] Plato, *Rep.* Lib. vi. 404.

LECTURE II.

ON THE PYRRHONIAN ETHIC.

"Τοῦτό μοι, ὦ Πύρρων, ἱμείρεται ἦτορ ἀκοῦσαι,
Πῶς ποτ' ἀνὴρ ἔτ' ἄγεις ῥᾷστα μεθ' ἡσυχίας,
Μοῦνος ἐν ἀνθρώποισι θεοῦ τρόπον ἡγεμονεύων."

§ *a*. SEXTUS EMPIRICUS in his Hypotyposes asserts that the name of Pyrrho had been rightly associated with the sceptical philosophy, from the fact that he above all his predecessors had systematised and developed its peculiar opinions. "Καὶ Πυρρώνειος ἀπὸ τοῦ φαίνεσθαι ἡμῖν τὸν Πύρρωνα σωματικώτερον καὶ ἐπιφανέστερον τῶν πρὸ αὐτοῦ προσεληλυθέναι τῇ σκέψει[1]." Let us now consider wherein consists the claim of Pyrrho to be recognised as the special founder of a new sect of philosophers. Scepticism, as a tendency of the human mind, must have been antecedent to the earliest efforts of man towards philosophical research, for doubt is as much the parent as the offspring of enquiry[2], and we find it appearing as a positive feature in one of the earliest manifestations of Greek speculation.

[1] *Hyp.* I. 3. 7.
[2] "Jeder tüchtigen Anfänger in der Philosophie ist Skeptiker. Und umgekehrt: jeder Skeptiker, *als solcher*, ist Anfänger."—Herbart, *Einleitung in die Philosophie*, chap. IV. p. 62.

Xenophanes of Colophon, the founder of the Eleatic school, had denied the possibility of attaining certain knowledge:

"δοκὸς δ' ἐπὶ πᾶσι τέτυκται[1]."

Socrates had recommended doubt as the best preparation of the mind for humble enquiry: "Ὦ Σώκρατες, ἤκουον μὲν ἔγωγε, πρὶν καὶ συγγενέσθαι σοι, ὅτι σὺ οὐδὲν ἄλλο ἢ αὐτός τε ἀπορεῖς, καὶ τοὺς ἄλλους ποιεῖς ἀπορεῖν. καὶ νῦν, ὥς γ' ἐμοὶ δοκεῖς, γοητεύεις με καὶ φαρμάττεις, καὶ ἀτεχνῶς κατεπάθεις, ὥστε μεστὸν ἀπορίας γεγονέναι[2]." Besides, Heraclitus, Democritus, Protagoras, and the whole of the Hedonistic school of philosophers, had implicitly or explicitly based their views of the relation of man to external nature on a sceptical method. Pyrrho then can scarcely be said in this respect to have introduced any novel system into the processes of philosophical investigation. Again, with regard to the avowed end of the Pyrrhonian doctrines, viz., the attainment of ἀταραξία[3], or a state of tranquil inaction as the *summum bonum* of a wise man[4], Socrates himself to a great degree, and the sect of Cynic philosophers had inculcated a life of contemplative virtue, as the proper end of a rational existence; and therefore Pyrrho cannot lay claim to originality in introducing this ascetic aim as the ultimate object of his whole philosophy. In what, we may ask, then did the

[1] *Hyp.* II. 4. 8.
[2] *Meno.* p. 80.
"ὅτι δὲ ἀτοπώτατός εἰμι καὶ ποιῶ τοὺς ἀνθρώπους ἀπορεῖν."
Theætetus, 149 *a*.
[3] Cicero refers this notion of ἀταραξία to Democritus. "Democriti autem securitas, quæ est animi tanquam tranquillitas, quam appellant εὐθυμίαν, eo seperanda fuit ab hac disputatione quia ista animi tranquillitas ea ipsa est beata vita."—*De Fin.* v. 8. Cf. Aristotle, *Eth. Nic.* II. 3. "Διὸ καὶ ὁρίζονται τὰς ἀρετὰς ἀπαθείας τινὰς καὶ ἠρεμίας."
[4] "τὸ μὲν μηδενὸς δεῖσθαι θεῖον εἶναι, τὸ δὲ ὡς ἐλαχίστων ἐγγυτάτω τοῦ θείου."
Xen. *Memor.* I. 6.

teaching of Pyrrho entitle him to the reputation of having founded a distinct school of philosophy? To this question we may reply: The distinguishing characteristic of Pyrrho's system was the employment of a sceptical method as an instrument for the attainment of virtue. Thus, in conformity with the tendency of the age, he attempted to unite speculative with practical philosophy; and, as Aristippus had deduced an art of life from the principles of subjective materialism—as Plato had endeavoured to found an ethical system on a basis of idealism—so Pyrrho in his turn essayed to solve the great problem of happiness by the aid of scepticism. It is, therefore, this aspect of Pyrrhonism to which we shall first direct our attention; constituting, as we think it does, a manifestation of human thought novel amongst its contemporaries, and unique amongst subsequent phases of opinion.

§ β. Every desire in the human mind implies also a belief in the existence of its object[1]. "Quod si aliquid aliquando acturus est, necesse est id ei verum, quod occurrit, videri." Lucullus, 8. This object is some quality or power in things to satisfy the appetite or feeling which has given rise to the desire. A belief in the existence of the object of desire, then, is a belief that the thing we desire is capable of producing an effect on us suitable to the feeling which prompted the desire. Hunger, for example, produces a desire for food, and we desire food because we believe that there exists in it a power to satisfy the cravings of hunger. Now in whatever way we may define that state of mind

[1] " ἥ τε γὰρ φιλαργυρία ὑπόληψίς ἐστι τοῦ τὸ ἀργύριον καλὸν εἶναι καὶ ἡ μέθη δὲ καὶ ἡ ἀκολασία ὁμοίως καὶ τἄλλα."—Diog. L. VII. 110 sqq.

" Quamobrem simul objecta species cujuspiam est, quod bonum videatur ad id adipiscendum impellit ipsa natura."—*Tus. Dis.* IV. 6. Kant's definition makes desire create its own object. "Begehrungsvermögen ist das Vermögen durch seine Vorstellungen Ursache der Gegenstande dieser Vorstellungen zu seyn."—*Einleitung in die Metaphysik der Sitten*, I. p. 9.

called belief, it is at any rate certain that such a state of mind is utterly opposed to, and incompatible with, that condition of consciousness we denominate doubt. Where there is doubt, there can at the same time be no belief. If belief, then, in the existence of the object of desire is a constitutive element of the desire itself, it is evident that any means employed to induce a state of doubt in the mind must have the effect of suppressing desire. Again, any determination of the mind to action, or act of volition, implies a previous presence of some desire or motive directing the will to some definite object[1]. It is true that every desire is not necessarily followed by action, but it is equally certain that every voluntary action must have been preceded by some desire.

Here then we have the central notion of the Pyrrhonian system, viz. to collect conflicting evidence concerning the reality of external objects, or the qualities of external objects[2]. By this means a feeling of doubt ($\dot{a}\pi o\rho\acute{\iota}a$) as to this reality is established in the mind, hence desire for the object is suppressed, and there being no incentive to effort, a state of inaction, or $\dot{a}\tau a\rho a\xi\acute{\iota}a$, ensues. "Alterum est, quod negatis actionem ullius rei posse in eo esse, qui nullam rem assensu suo comprobet. Primum enim videri oportet in quo sit etiam assensus. Dicunt enim Stoici, sensus ipsos assensus esse: quos quoniam appetitio consequatur, actionem sequi. Tolli autem omnia, si visa tollantur[3]." "For," says Sextus Empiricus[4], "he who believes that anything is *really* ($\phi\acute{v}\sigma\epsilon\iota$[5]) good

---

[1] "In all determinations of the mind that are of any importance, there must be something in the preceding state of the mind that disposes or inclines us to that determination."— Reid, "On the Active Powers of Man," Essay II. (Hamilton's *Reid*).

[2] Ἔστι δὲ ἡ σκεπτικὴ δύναμις ἀντιθετικὴ φαινομένων τε καὶ νοουμένων, κ.τ.λ. —*Hyp.* I. 4. 8.

[3] Lucullus, 33.   [4] *Hyp.* I. 12. 27—29—30.

[5] On this meaning of the word φύσει, see note on the Fabrician edition of Sextus Empiricus. (*Hyp.* I. 12. 27, note *l.*, p. 18). It is there translated by

or evil, is for ever being disturbed, and as long as those things he imagines good are not attained by him, he considers himself the victim of *real* evils, and he pursues eagerly those things he thinks are *really* good. But the attainment of them only leads him to further disquietude, because he is unreasonably and immoderately elated, and because dreading any change he strives his utmost to prevent these supposed benefits escaping him[1]. While on the contrary he who doubts concerning the *reality* of that which he considers good or evil, neither vehemently pursues, nor precipitately shuns anything, and therefore remains calm and tranquil[2]." "Now," continues Sextus Empiricus, "the Sceptics at first hoped to attain tranquillity by demonstrating the discrepancy between things perceived through the senses and those apprehended by the intellect; failing in this, they suspended their judgment (ἐπέσχον), and, as a necessary result, tranquillity followed this withholding of assent, as the shadow follows a body. Not that we mean to say a Sceptic is totally exempt from trouble; we admit he may

the Latin adverb *revera*. It seems to mean *really* or *by nature*, or *per se*, or any word which implies objective existence.

[1] "Ye Powers, why did you man create
   With such *insatiable* desire?
If you'd endow him with no more *estate*
   You should have made him *less aspire*.
But now our appetites you *Vex* and *Cheat*
   With *reall* Hunger, and *Phantastic* meat."
                        Norris' *Miscellany*. "The Complaint."

[2] Cf. "Partes autem perturbationum volunt ex duobus opinatis bonis nasci et ex duobus opinatis malis; ita esse quatuor. Ex bonis libidinem et laetitiam, ut sit laetitia praesentium bonorum, libido futurorum. Ex malis metum et aegritudinem nasci censent, metum futuris, aegritudinem praesentibus. Quae enim venientia metuuntur, eadem adficiunt aegritudine instantia. Laetitia autem et libido in bonorum opinione versantur: cum libido ad id, quod videtur bonum, illecta et inflammata rapiatur: laetitia ut adepta jam aliquid concupitum, efferatur et gestiat. Natura enim omnes ea, quae bona videntur, sequuntur fugiuntque contraria."—*Tusc. Disp.* IV. 6. Cf. Aristotle, *Eth. Nic.* II. 3.

suffer from thirst, cold, or any of the inevitable evils of life. But even under these circumstances, ordinary individuals are exposed to double suffering, both from the so-called evils themselves, and from believing them to be *essentially* evil. The Sceptic, dismissing the idea that there are any evils *per se*, endures them with fortitude. We say therefore that the aim of scepticism is inaction (ἀταραξία) under possible (δοξαστοῖς) circumstances; and moderate emotion (μετριοπάθειαν) under actual (κατηναγκασμένοις)." From these passages we are enabled to form some estimate of the scope and tendency of the Pyrrhonian teaching. Popularly stated, it was founded on the result of experience in common life; viz. that any good is greater in the anticipation, than in the enjoyment; and that evil is more in the dread, than in the suffering. In point of fact *man*, in virtue of the rational part of his nature, is more concerned with the future and possible, than with the present and actual. Hopes and fears are the levers of life, and the main incentives to all action. But on what are these hopes and fears grounded? Simply on our belief that the good and evil we see in things have an absolute and necessary existence. The poor man wishes to be rich. Why? Because he believes that the benefits to be derived from wealth are inherent in riches; he does not see that the happiness they confer is dependent on the susceptibilities of the possessor, and contingent on the circumstances which attend their possession. Health and strength of body, the attachment of friends, the affections of domestic life, may insure to him a much greater degree of happiness than is enjoyed by the rich man, to whom perhaps these accessories are wanting. Sextus E. mentions a forcible example of the effect of imagination in inducing a belief in the absolute and necessary nature of evil, instancing as a fact that, when witnessing a surgical operation performed on a friend, the bystander is often more overcome by the pain he *supposes* is being suffered than the patient is from the *actual* infliction. "'Ως μὲν γὰρ ἄνθρωπος αἰσθητικὸς πάσχει, μὴ προσδοξάζων δὲ ὅτι τοῦτο ὃ πάσχει κακόν ἐστι φύσει μετριοπαθεῖ· τὸ γὰρ προσδοξάζειν τι τοιοῦτο χεῖρόν ἐστι καὶ αὐτοῦ τοῦ πάσχειν, ὡς ἐνίοτε τοὺς μὲν τεμνομένους ἢ ἄλλο τι τοιοῦτο πάσχοντας φέρειν, τοὺς δὲ παρεστῶτας διὰ τὴν περὶ τοῦ γινομένου δόξαν ὡς φαύλου λειποψυχεῖν[1]." If then we admit that a life of tranquillity, of freedom from unrest and disquiet, should be the aim of a wise man, we cannot impugn the validity of the means the Pyrrhonists proposed for attaining that object. They cut at the root of all human hopes, fears, and desires, and left man in the possession solely of that consciousness of the present and actual which we suppose him to share with the brute creation. "Ergo hi, qui negant quidquam posse comprehendi, hæc ipsa eripiunt, vel instrumenta, vel ornamenta vitæ: vel potius etiam totam vitam evertunt funditus, ipsumque animal orbant animo[2]." Whether such a result, if it were possible, would be worthy the aspirations of an intelligent being we will leave for the present to the judgment of the reader. Sextus E. gives a characteristic summary of the Pyrrhonian reasoning on this subject, the conclusiveness of which seems at any rate not to have been doubted by him. "Ὅθεν ἐπιλογιζόμεθα ὅτι, εἰ τὸ κακοῦ ποιητικὸν, κακόν ἐστι καὶ φευκτόν, ἡ δὲ πεποίθησις τοῦ τάδε μὲν εἶναι φύσει ἀγαθὰ τάδε δὲ κακά, ταραχὰς ποιεῖ· κακόν ἐστι καὶ φευκτὸν τὸ ὑποτίθεσθαι καὶ πεποιθέναι φαῦλόν τι ἢ ἀγαθὸν ὡς πρὸς τὴν φύσιν εἶναι[3]."

[1] *Hyp.* III. 24. 236.   [2] Lucullus, 10.
[3] *Hyp.* III. 24. 238. The following reflections of M. Crousaz seem to embody the really common-sense view of the main aim of Pyrrhonism, viz. the attainment of tranquillity, and absence of all disquietude. "Le But dont les Sceptiques tiroient leur gloire renfermoit donc une contradiction palpable. L'ignorance où je suis sur la vérité ou sur la réalité de ce qui paroît Bien, et de ce qui paroit Mal, m'empêche d'être agité de Désirs et de Craintes,

§ γ. Of course we should not expect that a philosopher who considered the great end and aim of virtue to be the suppression of all incentives to action, would devote much attention to establishing any rules for the guidance of action. Pyrrho (and Aristo), says Cicero[1], insisted that every thing was comprised in virtue alone, to such a degree as to deprive it of all power of making any selection of external circumstances: "Enim in una virtute sic omnia esse voluerunt; ut eam rerum selectione exspoliarent[2]." Even a Pyrrhonist, although he might be able to subdue all motives to voluntary action, could not always resist the force of external circumstances, obeying them, however, as they said, simply in order not to oppose, following them without any inclination or proclivity, as a boy does his master, "τὸ γὰρ πείθεσθαι λέγεται διαφόρως, τό τε μὴ ἀντιτείνειν, ἀλλ' ἁπλῶς ἕπεσθαι ἄνευ σφοδρᾶς προσκλίσεως καὶ προσπαθείας, ὡς ὁ παῖς λέγεται πείθεσθαι τῷ παιδαγωγῷ[3], κ.τ.λ." Since then the Pyrrhonists admitted that they could not always remain inactive, they found it expedient to enunciate a standard of conduct according to which certain things were to be done, and certain others left undone. We say then, writes Sextus E.[4], that the criterion of life according to the scep-

et m'affermit dans une tranquillité inébranlable. Voilà mon but, disoient-ils. C'est tout le contraire leur dira une personne qui raisonne de bonne foy: car ignorant si mon état présent tournera à mon avantage, ou à mon malheur: ne connoissant aucun moien sûr pour me rendre heureux, ni pour me garantir de misère, qu'est ce qui me rassurera contra la Crainte? Pour vivre au dessus de la Crainte, ce n'est pas assés de savoir que le Mal pourroit n'arriver pas. Il faut que je sache du moins très vraisemblement qu'il n'arrivera pas. Il y a plus, car dans l'Hypothèse des Sceptiques, cette Proposition, *Peut-être qu'il n'arrivera pas du mal*, est en elle-même incertaine, et celle-ci, Peut-être m'est il impossible de l'éviter, n'est pas moins croyable. Un homme est-il au-dessus de la Crainte, lorsque, par la situation où la Philosophie a mis son esprit, cette Proposition, *Peut-être n'eviterai-je point les plus grands malheurs?* est pour lui aussi vraisemblable qu'aucune autre. Il faut être bien abruti, pour tenir contre cette Idée.—*Examen du Pyrrhonisme*, Part ii. Sec. 2, p. 67.

[1] *De Fin.* ii. 13. [2] *De Fin.* iv. 16, et passim.
[3] *Hyp.* i. 33. 230. [4] *Hyp.* i. 11. 21—22—23—24.

tical philosophy, is the apparent and actual (τὸ φαινόμενον), as a perception of a representative image in the mind (δυνάμει τὴν φαντασίαν αὐτοῦ οὕτω καλοῦντες). We live then, continues Sextus E., guided by the phenomenal manifestations around us (τοῖς φαινομένοις προσέχοντες), and consistently with the general order of nature (κατὰ τὴν βιωτικὴν τήρησιν¹). Now this consistency has reference to four regulative principles:

(1) Natural instinct (ἐν ὑφηγήσει φύσεως²), according to which we think and feel naturally.
(2) The impulse of appetite (ἀνάγκῃ παθῶν), by which hunger leads to food, thirst to drink.
(3) The authority of laws and customs (ἐν παραδόσει νόμων τε καὶ ἐθῶν), by which we are led to acknowledge that to live virtuously is good, to live viciously evil.
(4) The inductions of experience (ἐν διδασκαλίᾳ τεχνῶν), by which we advance in those arts we have undertaken to cultivate.

It is difficult to conceive how any criterion of action could have been derived from such principles as these. But in fact the most elevated systems of heathen morality, or at any rate those of the Empiric schools, did not seek any higher sources for rules of conduct. The '*summum bonum*' was at best but a conception generalized from the results of experience, i. e. *common sense;* from the suggestions of appetite, i.e. the *law* of *nature,* the end of desire, as Cicero calls it, '*extremum expetendi*³.' But it was this very

---

¹ Hence the lines of Timon:
"ἦ γὰρ ἐγὼν ἐρέω ὥς μοι καταφαίνεται εἶναι,
μῦθον ἀληθείης ὀρθὸν ἔχων κανόνα·
ὡς ἡ τοῦ θείου τε φύσις καὶ τἀγαθοῦ αἰεί
ἐξ ὧν ἰσότατος γίνεται ἀνδρὶ βίος."
                Sextus E., *Adv. Math.* xi. 20.
² *Hyp.* i. 11. 23.   ³ Lucullus, 9.

conception, or *'summum bonum,'* in which the distinction lay between the sceptical and dogmatical moralists ; for while the latter, from observations of the intentions of nature[1], established principles of action which might guide them to live in accordance with her laws, the former, rejecting the validity of such inductions, on the ground of the uncertainty of all things, would not admit any rule of life but such as could be immediately deduced from the circumstances of the present, and the exigencies of our natural appetites.

Against the possibility of there being any absolute standard of good or evil the Pyrrhonists were most vehement in their attacks[2]. The greater part of the chapter on ethics in the work of Sextus E. is devoted to this subject, and the whole armoury of sceptical logic is ransacked for arguments in support of their general assertion, viz. that if there were any absolute good or evil it would appear the same to all. We will extract a brief summary of the Pyrrhonian reasonings on this subject from the writings of Diogenes Laertius[3]. Pyrrho (says he) used to affirm that nothing was honourable or disgraceful, just or unjust; and on the same principle he (Pyrrho) said there was no such thing as downright truth, but that man did everything in consequence of custom or law.

For that nothing was any more this than that. The same thing is just in the case of some people and unjust in that of others. If there be any natural good, or any natural evil, then it must be good to everyone, or evil to everyone, just as snow is cold to everyone. But there is no such thing as one general good or evil common to all beings. Therefore there is no such thing as natural good, or natural evil, for either

---

[1] "Cum omnium artium is finis esset, quid natura maxime quæreret, idem statui debere de totius arte vitæ."—*De Fin.* IV. 8.
[2] *Hyp.* III. chap. 23.
[3] Diogenes Laertius, IX. 61—83—90—101.

one must pronounce everything good which is thought so by
anyone whatever, or one must say that it does not follow
that everything which is thought good is good. Now we
cannot say that everything which is thought good is good,
since the same thing is thought good by one person (as for
instance pleasure is thought good by Epicurus) and evil by
another (as it is thought evil by Antisthenes); and on this
principle the same thing will be both good and evil[1].

Again, we assert that it does not follow that everything
which is thought good is good. Then we must distinguish
between the different opinions, which it is not possible to do,
by reason of the equality of the reasons adduced in support
of each. It follows then that we cannot recognise anything
as good by nature. Such are the logical consequences of an
empirical ethology, where happiness is the criterion of life,
and reason the arbiter of happiness. For can the purely
subjective and apparent furnish any immutable principles of
morality, unless the existence of some internal sense is
admitted by which a natural distinction in things can be
perceived? Such an innate principle the adversaries of the
Sceptics would not allow, hence the morality of Pyrrhonism,
however low and unsatisfactory it may have been, was really
only the inevitable result of the rejection of all *a priori*
sources of knowledge. It may have been merely to support
this conclusion that Pyrrho, and afterwards the New Academicians, proclaimed the contingent and arbitrary nature of all
distinction between right and wrong. The idea of laws in

---

[1] "The language about the good and the base is the ordinary language
of sceptical despair. Such despair being compatible with the belief that
anything is possible because nothing is true."—Maurice, *Moral and Metaphysical Philosophy*, Chap. VI. Div. 4, Sec. II. p. 212.

"Dass er allen Unterschied von Gut und Böse, Gerecht und Ungerecht,
geläugnet und nur Sitte und Gesetz als Richtschnur unsrer Handlungen
anerkannt habe, ist wohl als Folgerung aus seiner Behauptung von der
Unerkennbarkeit der Dinge zu betrachten."—Brandis, *Geschichte der Entwickelungen der Griechischen Philosophie*, Vol. II. p. 177.

the moral constitution of man, which modern philosophers have substituted for purely objective reasons in things, was not yet understood by the ancient Greek moralists. There seemed therefore no alternative between Platonism and Empiricism; and since the latter was the prevailing tendency of the post-Aristotelian philosophy, its data were of course the groundwork of scepticism. We have now glanced at some of the main features of the Pyrrhonian ethic. As a basis for an art of life it was simply impossible. If we are to believe the anecdotes in Diogenes Laertius it would appear to have required all the care of Pyrrho's friends to prevent him being a victim of his own principles.

But we do not imagine his doctrines had many votaries. Sextus Empiricus states[1] that the later Sceptics abandoned the idea of ἀταραξία as the end of their philosophy, and Cicero tells us that in his day Pyrrhonism had long since fallen into oblivion, "Nam Pyrrho, Aristo, Herillus, jam diu abjecti[2]." "Jam explosæ ejectæque sententiæ Pyrrhonis, etc.[3]" In our next Lecture we shall proceed to the consideration of the purely sceptical side of the Pyrrhonian philosophy, constituting as it does by far the greater portion of the treatise of Sextus Empiricus.

[1] *Hyp.* I. 12. 30.   [2] *De Fin.* II. 11.
[3] *De Fin.* v. 8.

LECTURE III.

ON THE GROUNDS OF SCEPTICISM.

"τοῖς μὲν γὰρ ἤδη, τοῖς δ' ἐν ὑστέρῳ χρόνῳ
τὰ τερπνὰ πικρὰ γίγνεται καὖθις φίλα."

§ *a.* EVERY perception is a modification or change of our consciousness, an effect of the joint operation of some power in the external object causing the perception, and some degree of susceptibility in the mind of the perceiving subject.[1] Now, if the same object when brought *alone*

---

[1] We are not attributing here any special theory of cognition to the Sceptic. As we shall have frequent occasion to remark, scepticism is always founded on the dogmas of its adversaries. We have only attempted to catch the crude notion of perception which seemed to have been assumed by the sceptical philosophers, where the physical and metaphysical, logical and psychological points of view are interchanged and confused. As a proof of this compare the exposition of the same subject by a modern metaphysician. "Consciousness presents itself as the product of two factors, *I* and *something*. The problem of the unconditioned is, briefly stated, to reduce these two factors to one. For it is manifest that, so long as they remain two, we have no unconditioned, but a pair of conditioned existences. If the *something* of which I am conscious is a separate reality, having qualities and modes of action of its own, and thereby determining, or contributing to determine, the form which my consciousness of it may take, my consciousness is thereby conditioned, or partly dependent on something beyond itself. It is no matter, in this respect, whether the influence is direct or indirect—whether, for instance, I see a material tree, or only the mental image of a tree. If the

into connection with the perceiving subject always produced the *same* percept, we might argue that the sensibility of the subject was constant, and that the percept was a measure, so to speak, of the power of the object. Again, if the object being brought *not alone*, but together with others, into connection with the percipient subject, produced the *same* percept, we should say that the power of the object was absolute, necessary, and independent of contingent circumstances; and still we might continue to assert that the percept was a measure, as it were, of the power of the object.

Now with regard to the phenomenon of perception as taking place momentarily in ourselves, experience tells us that neither of the hypotheses mentioned above is true. For the same object *alone* does not always produce the same percept, nor does it when accompanied by different circumstances. The inference therefore is that,

1. The mental susceptibility varies in the subject, and therefore that the power of the object is manifested in the percept, not *absolutely*, but only *relatively*.

2. That the power of the object is dependent upon circumstances extraneous to the percipient subject, and is therefore only manifested in the percept relatively to those circumstances.

From these considerations the Sceptics argued that we

---

nature of the thing in any degree determines the character of the image—if the visible form of a tree is different from that of a house because the tree itself is different from the house, my consciousness is, however remotely, influenced by something different from itself, the *ego* by the *non-ego*. And on the other hand, if I, who am conscious, am a real being, distinct from the things of which I am conscious—if the conscious mind has a constitution and laws of its own by which it acts, and if the mode of its consciousness is in any degree determined by those laws, the *non-ego* is so far conditioned by the *ego*; the thing which I see is not seen absolutely, and *per se*, but in a form partly dependent upon the laws of my vision."—Mansel, *The Philosophy of the Conditioned*, pp. 4—6.

could not predicate of any given object what percept it would produce in the mind, and conversely, from any percept the object which had caused it. Now, as we have already seen, a belief in the capacity of known objects to produce constant effects is a necessary element of those states of mind we call hopes, fears, and desires, which are the antecedents of action. "Quare qui aut visum, aut assensum tollit, is omnem actionem tollit e vita[1]." Again, a belief in our ability to recognize an object from our perception of its effect on the mind is what we call knowledge[2], and the degree of certitude which this knowledge possesses is proportional to the degree of this belief. But it is obvious that the degree of confidence with which we can assign any absolute power or property to an object must depend upon the amount of faith we accord to the testimony of those perceptions by which we originally discriminated the existence of these qualities. Now what is the nature of this testimony, and how far are we justified in granting it our assent? A, B, and C, we will say, are about to form a judgment on some quality of an object perceived by the sense of taste. A, judging by the testimony of his consciousness, pronounces the object to be sweet, B perhaps says that it has no taste at all, and C that it is even bitter[3]. Now here are three conflicting decisions on the same fact; how are we to tell which of them is true? Is there any absolute and permanent quality in the object causing our perception of sweetness? Surely we could not say so, on such evidence; appearances there may be. Three different appearances, says the Sceptic, and the existence of these I will believe; but what am I to infer from the discrepancy of

---
[1] Lucullus, 12.
[2] "Knowledge implies three things: 1. Firm Belief; 2. Of what is true; 3. On sufficient grounds."—Whately, *Logic*, Book IV. chap. 2, note 13.
[3] Cf. Lucretius, IV. 658:
"hoc ubi quod suave est aliis, aliis fit amarum."

their deliverances as to the real nature of the external object. Heraclitus answers that the same thing is *both* sweet and bitter. "*καὶ οἱ μὲν Σκεπτικοὶ φαίνεσθαι λέγουσι τὰ ἐναντία περὶ τὸ αὐτό, οἱ δὲ Ἡρακλείτειοι ἀπὸ τούτου καὶ ἐπὶ τὸ ὑπάρχειν αὐτὰ μετέρχονται*[1]." Democritus denied reality of existence to everything but space and atoms, declaring that all the other attributes of matter were but apparent and phenomenal. "*ἀπὸ γὰρ τοῦ τοῖς μὲν γλυκὺ φαίνεσθαι τὸ μέλι, τοῖς δὲ πικρόν, τὸν Δημόκριτον ἐπιλογίζεσθαί φασι τὸ μήτε γλυκὺ αὐτὸ εἶναι μήτε πικρόν*[2]." Protagoras the Sophist declared his opinion on the limit of reality in the well-known aphorism, "*πάντων χρημάτων εἶναι μέτρον τὸν ἄνθρωπον*[3]." Meaning that we could affirm existence of nothing but our momentary sensations, a simple relation between subject and object, "*τίθησι τὰ φαινόμενα ἑκάστῳ μόνα, καὶ οὕτως εἰσάγει τὸ πρός τι*[4]." The Cyrenaics, extending this doctrine, maintained that they only properly perceived those things which they felt by their inmost touch, such as pain or pleasure. "Quid Cyrenaei videntur? minime contempti philosophi, qui negant esse quidquam, quod percipi possit extrinsecus: ea se sola percipere, quæ tactu intimo sentiant, ut dolorem, ut voluptatem: neque se, quo quid colore aut quo sono sit, scire, sed tantum sentire, affici se quodam modo[5]." Thus we see, from the uncertainty attaching to the reports of sense, philosophers concluded that the real nature of things must be very different from that

---

[1] *Hyp.* I. 29—210.
[2] *Hyp.* I. 30. 213. "Δημόκριτος δὲ ὅτι μὲν ἀναιρεῖ τὰ φαινόμενα ταῖς αἰσθήσεσι, καὶ τούτων λέγει μηδὲν φαίνεσθαι κατὰ ἀλήθειαν ἀλλὰ μόνον κατὰ δόξαν· ἀληθὲς δὲ ἐν τοῖς οὖσιν ὑπάρχειν τὸ ἀτόμους εἶναι καὶ κενόν· 'νόμῳ γὰρ' φησί 'γλυκὺ καὶ νόμῳ πικρόν, νόμῳ θερμόν, νόμῳ ψυχρόν, νόμῳ χροιή, ἐτεῇ δὲ ἄτομα καὶ κενόν.'"—*Adv. Math.* VII. 135.
"τῶν δ' ἄλλων αἰσθητῶν οὐδενὸς εἶναι φύσιν, ἀλλὰ πάντα πάθη τῆς αἰσθήσεως ἀλλοιουμένης, ἐξ ἧς γίνεσθαι τὴν φαντασίαν. κ.τ.λ."—Theophr. *de Sensu*, 63.
[3] *Hyp.* I. 32, 216. [4] *l. l.* 216. [5] Lucullus, 24.

which the common convictions of mankind ascribed to them. But still we observe that, although commencing by doubting that which the majority of mankind believe, many of the early thinkers ended by believing much that the majority of mankind would doubt. They in fact drew dogmatic conclusions from sceptical premises.

§ β. The Pyrrhonists did not fail to detect the inconsistency in the reasonings of their predecessors, and while proclaiming the untrustworthiness of all knowledge founded on the evidence of sense, declared that this very uncertainty rendered it impossible to posit any dogma concerning things beyond our immediate consciousness (τὰ ἄδηλα). Thus they maintained a consistent attitude of doubt respecting everything but the subjective phenomena revealed in perception. "τὰ γὰρ κατὰ φαντασίαν παθητικὰ[1] ἀβουλήτως ἡμᾶς ἄγοντα εἰς συγκατάθεσιν οὐκ ἀνατρέπομεν,—ταῦτα δέ ἐστι τὰ φαινόμενα, ὅταν δὲ ζητῶμεν εἰ τοιοῦτόν ἐστι τὸ ὑποκείμενον, ὁποῖον φαίνεται, τὸ μὲν ὅτι φαίνεται δίδομεν, ζητοῦμεν δ' οὐ περὶ τοῦ φαινομένου, ἀλλὰ περὶ ἐκείνου ὃ λέγεται περὶ τοῦ φαινομένου.—οἷον φαίνεται ἡμῖν γλυκάζειν τὸ μέλι· τοῦτο συγχωροῦμεν· γλυκαζόμεθα γὰρ αἰσθητικῶς. εἰ δὲ καὶ γλυκύ ἐστιν ὅσον ἐπὶ τῷ λόγῳ, ζητοῦμεν· ὃ οὐκ ἔστι τὸ φαινόμενον, ἀλλὰ περὶ τοῦ φαινομένου λεγόμενον[2]." From this passage it is apparent that the Pyrrhonists regarded our knowledge as extending no further than the perception of one term of a ratio, which afforded no evidence as to the nature of its correlative. Of course the maintenance of such a position as this, a position opposed to the natural convictions of humanity, would really depend upon the ability of its supporters to shake the common faith in the veracity of consciousness, by adducing a multitude of proofs as jus-

[1] For meaning of the word παθητικός, see Hamilton's *Reid*, note D. (note on paragraph 6).
[2] *Hyp.* I. 10. 19, 20.

tification of their own scepticism. Accordingly Pyrrho enunciated the celebrated δέκα τρόποι, or τόποι, ten presumptions derived from a consideration of the circumstances under which our commerce with the objects of external nature takes place. From these reasons he argued that the relation between the object and subject is probably so variable and contingent, that from the subjective phenomena of our consciousness we can affirm nothing certain, either through the evidence of sense or the conclusions of reason.

These considerations the Pyrrhonists verified by a mass of examples drawn from observation and experience, and they are therefore the facts *upon* the *truth* of which must mainly depend the validity of their whole method. We will briefly narrate these ten grounds, together with a few examples of each. They will afford the reader a glimpse of the kind of reasoning ancient philosophers did not think unworthy of advancing in support of their own views.

1. The *first* ground of doubt is derived from a consideration of the variety observable in the physical organisation of animals (παρὰ τὴν τῶν ζῴων ἐξαλλαγήν[1]).

For according to the different constitutions of animals, their senses, or faculties of judging and perceiving, may be supposed to vary.

In confirmation of this presumption instances are adduced where, when the organs of sight, taste, smell etc., have been abnormally deranged, the apprehensions which we derive through them appear to suffer alteration. For example, writes Sextus Empiricus, they who have the jaundice say that those things are yellow which appear white to us, and they whose eyes are bloodshot affirm them to be red. Now some animals have their eyes yellow, others bloodshot, others whitish, and others different colours. It is therefore probable that the conception of colour is different in the

[1] *Hyp.* I. 14. 36.

case of these animals (εἰκὸς οἶμαι διάφορον αὐτοῖς τὴν τῶν χρωμάτων ἀντίληψιν γίγνεσθαι¹). Again, a concave mirror shews the object it reflects as smaller than reality, and one that is convex, as narrower, and more elongated; and some reflect the head of the observer downwards, with his feet upwards. Now since the eyes of some animals protrude, while those of others are sunken, of others flat, it is probable that the images of external objects vary for this reason, and that dogs, fish, lions, men and grasshoppers do not see the same things as equal in size, or alike in form, but that the vision receives the object, and makes an image corresponding to the faculty of each, (οἵαν ἑκάστου ποιεῖ τύπωσιν ἡ δεχομένη τὸ φαινόμενον ὄψις²). Again, with the sense of taste when the tongue is parched and dry, as in fever, we seem to taste everything bitter and earthy. We experience this in consequence of the different degree of moisture pervading us; and since some animals have a variety of tasting organs, and are full of different humours, they would naturally receive different impressions through the sense of taste. In fine, as the *same* food being administered turns to a vein in one place, to an artery in another, to a bone here, a nerve there, and to each of the other parts of the body evinces a variety of capabilities according to the susceptibility of the parts which receive it; as also water given to plants although of *one* and the *same* kind, in one place becomes bark, in another branches, in another fruit, now a fig, now an apple, etc.; as the breath of a musician, although *one* and the *same*, when breathed into the flute is sometimes sharp, and sometimes deep; and as the *same* touch of the hand on the lyre may produce both a shrill and a dull tone, so it is probable that external objects may be perceived differently according to the constitution of the percipient subject (εἰκὸς καὶ τὰ ἐκτὸς ὑποκείμενα διάφορα

[1] *l. l.* 44.   [2] *l. l.* 49.

θεωρεῖσθαι παρὰ τὴν διάφορον κατασκευὴν τῶν τὰς φαντασίας ὑπομενόντων ζώων[1]).

2. The *second* ground considers the variety in the constitution of men (παρὰ τὴν τῶν ἀνθρώπων διαφοράν[2]). Man, says Sextus Empiricus, has a twofold nature, sensuous and intellectual. In virtue of the former, as was shown in the case of animals, it is probable that differences of constitution would produce differences in the perception of the same external object, or qualities of an object. Again with regard to his mind the variety in desires and aversions has been the theme of poets in all ages[3]. Now, continues Sextus Empiricus, since desire and aversion originate in pleasure and pain, and pleasure and pain depend upon sense and perception, inasmuch as one seeks and another avoids the same thing, it is easy to conclude that all are not affected in the *same* way by the *same* object. If they were they would all desire the *same* thing. But if the same things affect men differently according to their different susceptibilities we should consider this sufficient ground for suspending our judgment. Each one is able to pronounce from his own point of view how an object appears to him, but no one can determine what is the real power or nature of anything (ὅ τι μὲν ἕκαστον φαίνεται τῶν ὑποκειμένων, ὡς πρὸς ἑκάστην διαφορὰν ἴσως λέγειν ἡμῶν δυναμένων· τί δέ ἐστι κατὰ δύναμιν ὡς πρὸς τὴν φύσιν οὐχ οἴων τε ὄντων ἀποφήνασθαι)[4].

3. The *third* occasion of doubt is found in the different

---

[1] *l. l.* 55.   [2] *l. l.* 36.
[3] ὁ μὲν γὰρ Πίνδαρός φησι·
"'Ἀελλοπόδων μέν τιν' εὐφραίνοισιν ἵππων
τίμια καὶ στέφανοι, τοὺς δ' ἐν πολυχρύσοις θαλάμοις βιοτά·
τέρπεται δὲ καί τις ἐπ' οἶδμ' ἅλιον ναΐ θοᾷ
σῶς διαστείβων."—Cf. Horace, lib. I. Ode 1.
"ὁ δὲ ποιητὴς λέγει
ἄλλοις γάρ τ' ἄλλοισιν ἀνὴρ ἐπιτέρπεται ἔργοις."—*Odyss.* ξ. 228.
Πυρ. I. 14. 86.
[4] *l. l.* 87.

functions of the organs of sense (παρὰ τὰς διαφόρους τῶν αἰσθητηρίων κατασκευάς)[1]. Each organ of sense seems to indicate to us a separate quality in the external object. An apple, for example, appears smooth to the touch, fragrant to the smell, sweet to the taste, and of a certain colour to the sight. But how do we know that it has really more than one quality, and that this apparent diversity is not due to the various capabilities of our organs of sense? For, as we have previously remarked, the same breath produces different notes on the same instrument, and the same nourishment is differently appropriated according to the different parts of the body to which it is assimilated. Again, can we assert that these are the only qualities of an apple? Let us imagine, for instance, a man who from his birth has possessed but the sense of touch, of taste, and of smell. This man would not be able to conceive the existence of such qualities as affect the sense of sight and of hearing. It may happen, then, that having only five senses we are unable to detect qualities which may yet really be in the apple. Since then there is no absurdity in saying that the different qualities we think we may perceive in an apple are inherent in it, and many more besides perhaps, or, on the contrary, that there is in reality only one cause in the object which produces different effects according to the diversity in our organs of sense, we cannot state with certainty the nature of this apple. Now if external objects are incomprehensible through the senses we cannot assuredly judge of them by the reason; therefore we ought to suspend our judgment (τῶν αἰσθήσεων μέν τοι μὴ καταλαμβανουσῶν τὰ ἐκτός, οὐδὲ ἡ διάνοια ταῦτα δύναται καταλαμβάνειν. ὥστε καὶ διὰ τοῦτον τὸν λόγον ἡ περὶ τῶν ἐκτὸς ὑποκειμένων ἐποχὴ συνάγεσθαι δόξει)[2].

4. The *fourth* reason for doubt is found in the subjective circumstances under which objects are perceived (παρὰ τὰς

[1] *l. l.* 86.   [2] *l. l.* 99.

περιστάσεις[1]). The condition of the body or mind of the percipient subject has great effect in modifying the impressions received from external objects. As has been already noticed, a person in sickness detects a different smell, taste, or colour in things from one in health; strong mental emotions also are well known to influence the ideas we receive from objects[2]. Of course it is an obvious rejoinder to arguments drawn from this source, that the Sceptics have no right to bring the discrepancy of perceptions received in an abnormal state of the body or mind as evidence against the veracity of those we have in our natural state. To this, however, Sextus Empiricus replies, that for such an objection to be of any value we ought to have some good reason for supposing that the impressions we receive in health are more trustworthy reports of external qualities than those of sickness or delirium. Now, continues Sextus Empiricus, he who considers the perceptions of a man in one state more trustworthy than those of a man in another, either makes this preference after proof and demonstration, or without proof and demonstration. In the *latter* case one would certainly not believe him, and in the *former*, one could scarcely afford him much more credit. For if he is going to prove to us the veracity of his perceptions he must employ some criterion or standard of their truth (εἰ γὰρ κρινεῖ τὰς φαντασίας, πάντως κριτηρίῳ κρινεῖ)[3]. But he must also be convinced that the criterion itself is trustworthy, for if it is false it is of no value as a measure of truth. Now if he maintains this criterion to be reliable, he must either do so after proof and demonstration, or without proof and demonstration. If the *former*, he is not worthy of credit, if the *latter*, he must show that his proof

[1] *l. l.* 36.
[2] "Οἷος δὲ καὶ τὴν ὄψιν εἶναι φαίνεται
ἀφ' οὗ τοιοῦτος γέγονεν, οἷον θηρίον.
τὸ μηδὲν ἀδικεῖν καὶ καλοὺς ἡμᾶς ποιεῖ."—*l. l.* 108.
[3] *l. l.* 114.

III.] *THE GROUNDS OF SCEPTICISM.* 49

and demonstration are conclusive. But here again he will require a criterion by which to measure the truth of his demonstration; but the truth of this criterion will again require demonstration, and so on, "every criterion a demonstration," and "every demonstration a criterion." For neither is the demonstration true, but in virtue of the truth of the criterion, or the criterion, except in virtue of the truth of the demonstration. Thus, when we try to prove the truth of the *demonstration* by the truth of the *criterion*, and the truth of the *criterion* by the truth of the *demonstration*, we fall into the sophistical circle, which we call the diallel (χρήζει γὰρ ἀεὶ καὶ ἡ ἀπόδειξις κριτηρίου, ἵνα βεβαιωθῇ, καὶ τὸ κριτήριον ἀποδείξεως, ἵνα ἀληθὲς εἶναι δειχθῇ. καὶ οὔτε ἀπόδειξις ὑγιὴς εἶναι δύναται, μὴ προϋπάρχοντος κριτηρίου ἀληθοῦς, οὔτε κριτήριον ἀληθές, μὴ προπεπιστευμένης τῆς ἀποδείξεως. καὶ οὕτως ἐμπίπτουσιν εἰς τὸν διάλληλον τρόπον τό τε κριτήριον καὶ ἡ ἀπόδειξις, ἐν ᾧ ἀμφότερα εὑρίσκεται ἄπιστα· ἑκάτερον γὰρ τὴν θατέρου πίστιν περιμένον ὁμοίως τῷ λοιπῷ ἐστιν ἄπιστον[1]).

5. The *fifth* ground refers to the difference in position, distance, and objective circumstances of things (παρὰ τὰς θέσεις καὶ τὰ διαστήματα καὶ τοὺς τόπους[2]). Any change in the relations of objects to one another, or to us, with respect to distance, or position, effects a change in their appearance. A colonnade[3] seen by an observer at one extremity, seems to narrow towards the other, but when seen from the middle, the breadth appears equal throughout. Again, the same tower appears round at a distance, square when near[4]. The blade of an oar appears broken in the water. The colour of the neck of a dove seems to vary as it turns. The light of

[1] *Hyp. l. l.* 116, 117.   [2] *l. l.* 36.
[3] "Uniformitas aequalissimae porticus acuitur in fine, dum acies in concluso stipata illis tenuatur, quo et extenditur."—Tertullian, *De Anima*, c. 17.
[4] "Quadratasque procul turris cum cernimus urbis,
    Propterea fit uti videantur saepe rotundae."—Lucretius, IV. 353, 4.

L. L.   4

a lamp is faint in the sun, brilliant in the shade. It may be urged of course that, of these manifestations, some are according to the true nature of the object, others not; to which the Sceptic replies, that it must then be demonstrated in which position, distance, or situation the real object is revealed, otherwise one is as good as another. This demonstration requires another demonstration to show that the result of the first is true, and so on, *usque ad infinitum*. Thus, although we may be able to say how an object appears to us in a certain position, or at a certain distance, we cannot assert what its absolute independent nature is (ὁποῖον μὲν φαίνεται ἕκαστον κατὰ τήνδε τὴν θέσιν ἢ κατὰ τόδε τὸ διάστημα ἢ ἐν τῷδε, εἰπεῖν ἴσως δυναμένων ἡμῶν, ὁποῖον δέ ἐστιν ὡς πρὸς τὴν φύσιν ἀδυνατούντων ἀποφαίνεσθαι διὰ τὰ προειρημένα[1]).

6. The *sixth* reason for doubting is founded on the complexity of objects (παρὰ τὰς ἐπιμιξίας[2]). We never can say any object is perceived alone simply and singly, but is always accompanied and modified by something extrinsic to itself, as air, light, moisture, cold, or heat. Thus, it is impossible to distinguish the real nature of anything, owing to the difficulty of separating it from contingent circumstances. The same body is heavy in the air, and light in the water. A tone sounds muffled and dull in a full room, which is clear and loud in a spacious apartment; and other examples analogous. Hence, in consequence of this complexity, the senses do not receive faithfully the qualities of external objects, and the reason cannot judge of them because she relies on the reports of the senses, and they are deceived (ὥστε διὰ τὰς ἐπιμιξίας αἱ αἰσθήσεις οὐκ ἀντιλαμβάνονται ὁποῖα πρὸς ἀκρίβειαν τὰ ἐκτὸς ὑποκείμενά ἐστιν. ἀλλ' οὐδὲ ἡ διάνοια· μάλιστα μὲν ἐπεὶ αἱ ὁδηγοὶ αὐτῆς αἰσθήσεις σφάλλονται[3]).

[1] *Hyp.* I. 14. 37.   [2] *l. l.* 134.   [3] *l. l.* 37.

7. The *seventh* ground of scepticism is derived from a consideration of the different proportions and ingredients of matter in objects (παρὰ τὰς ποσότητας καὶ σκευασίας τῶν ὑποκειμένων¹.) It is observed by the chemist if he mixes his drugs in a certain proportion, the resulting compound may be a restorative to health and strength, whereas more or less of one of the ingredients may cause the dose to be baneful, or even destructive. Thus the difference a slight alteration in the component elements of a substance makes in its qualities or powers, shows that we can only have an obscure notion of the real constitution of objects (οὕτως ὁ κατὰ τὰς ποσότητας καὶ σκευασίας λόγος συγχεῖ τὴν τῶν ἐκτὸς ὑποκειμένων ὕπαρξιν. διόπερ εἰκότως ἂν καὶ οὗτος ὁ τρόπος εἰς ἐποχὴν ἡμᾶς περιάγοι μὴ δυναμένους εἰλικρινῶς ἀποφήνασθαι περὶ τῆς φύσεως τῶν ἐκτὸς ὑποκειμένων²).

8. The *eighth* cause of doubt founds on the relativity of all things (ἀπὸ τοῦ πρός τι³). This τρόπος merely draws attention *to*, and places *in* a stronger light, the conclusions of the first seven. We have seen that the substance of the first four τρόποι is, the impossibility of arriving at a knowledge of the absolute nature of objects, because, to be perceived, implies a relation to a percipient subject. And again the fifth, sixth, and seventh τρόποι show, that as we never perceive anything singly, our notions of objects must always involve their relation to those which are perceived with them, therefore we cannot imagine anything which is unconditioned, either with respect to ourselves or anything else (πλὴν ἀλλ' οὕτω παραστάντων ἡμῶν ὅτι πάντα ἐστὶ πρός τι, δῆλόν ἐστι τὸ λοιπὸν ὅτι, ὁποῖόν ἐστιν ἕκαστον τῶν ὑποκειμένων κατὰ τὴν ἑαυτοῦ φύσιν καὶ εἰλικρινῶς λέγειν οὐ δυνησόμεθα, ἀλλ' ὁποῖον φαίνεται ἐν τῷ πρός τι· ἀκολουθεῖ τὸ περὶ τῆς φύσεως τῶν πραγμάτων δεῖν ἡμᾶς ἐπέχειν⁴).

[1] l. l. 37.
[2] l. l. 134.
[3] l. l. 37.
[4] l. l. 140.

9. The *ninth* mode rests on the frequency or rarity of the apparition of objects (παρὰ τὰς συνεχεῖς ἢ σπανίους ἐγκυρήσεις[1]).

The effect of objects on us is much modified by the conditions of time under which they occur. The sun (says Sextus E.) is, *per se*, a more wonderful object than a comet, but because we see a comet seldom, and the sun daily, the apparition of the former so affects our imagination that we believe it the forerunner of some special event[2]. Again, we value things which are rare, and view with indifference such as are easily attainable. If gold was as common as flint we should not covet it. Since then the same things appear precious or contemptible according as they are abundant or scarce, we conclude that we may be able to say how things appear to us when fettered with the conditions of time, but we cannot affirm what they are absolutely (ἐπεὶ οὖν τὰ αὐτὰ πράγματα παρὰ τὰς συνεχεῖς ἢ σπανίους περιπτώσεις ὁτὲ μὲν ἐκπληκτικὰ ἢ τίμια, ὁτὲ δὲ οὐ τοιαῦτα εἶναι δοκεῖ, ἐπιλογιζόμεθα ὅτι ὁποῖον μὲν φαίνεται τούτων ἕκαστον μετὰ συνεχοῦς περιπτώσεως ἢ σπανίας, ἴσως δυνησόμεθα λέγειν· ψιλᾶς δὲ ὁποῖον ἐστιν ἕκαστον τῶν ἐκτὸς ὑποκειμένων οὐκ ἐσμὲν δυνατοὶ φάσκειν[3]).

10. The *tenth* and last ground regards institutions, customs, laws, superstitious beliefs, and dogmatical opinions (παρὰ τὰς ἀγωγὰς, καὶ τὰ ἔθη, καὶ τοὺς νομούς, καὶ τὰς μυθικὰς πίστεις, καὶ τὰς δογματικὰς ὑπολήψεις[4]).

An institution is a certain standard of conduct in life, founded on the judgment of one man (as Diogenes), of a nation (as the Lacedæmonians). A law is a decree imposed

---

[1] *l. l.* 37.

[2] "Solis exortus, cursus, occasus nemo admiratur, propterea quod quotidie fiunt: at eclipses solis mirantur, quia raro accidunt: et solis eclipses magis mirantur, quam lunæ, quoniam hæ crebriores sunt."—Cicero, *ad Herennium*, 3. 22; Aristotle, *Meteorolog.*, lib. I. c. 7; Seneca, *Quæst.* 7. 28.

[3] *Hyp.* I. 11, 144.   [4] *l. l.* 37.

by the rulers of a state, the infraction of which involves the punishment of the transgressor. A custom is a convention arrived at by the unanimous consent of many, the violation of which does not entail punishment. A superstitious belief is the approbation accorded to legends of doubtful authenticity. A dogmatical conception is a conclusion deduced by the reason from given premisses[1]. In reference to these definitions the Sceptics adduced the facts, that that which was legal in one country was illegal in another. Similarly, that customs, institutions, and opinions vary among nations, among classes in the same nation, among sects of philosophers, and even among individuals. Hence it was to be concluded that the nature of objects, as far as regards their value and importance, their capacity of producing pleasure and pain—in short, all their effective qualities—is dependent upon the existence, or non-existence, of these artificial and arbitrary institutions. Therefore, we may be able to pronounce judgment on the attributes of objects as they are in relation to the established opinions of an age or country, but we cannot say what they are absolutely or necessarily (πλὴν τοσαύτης ἀνωμαλίας πραγμάτων καὶ διὰ τούτου τοῦ τρόπου δεικνυμένης, ὁποῖον μέν ἐστι τὸ ὑποκείμενον κατὰ τὴν φύσιν οὐχ ἕξομεν λέγειν, ὁποῖον δὲ φαίνεται πρὸς τήνδε τὴν ἀγωγήν, ἢ πρὸς τόνδε τὸν νόμον, ἢ πρὸς τόδε τὸ ἔθος καὶ τῶν ἄλλων ἕκαστον. καὶ διὰ τοῦτον οὖν περὶ τῆς φύσεως τῶν ἐκτὸς ὑποκειμένων πραγμάτων ἐπέχειν ἡμᾶς ἀνάγκη. οὕτω μὲν οὖν διὰ τῶν δέκα τρόπων καταλήγομεν εἰς τὴν ἐποχήν[2]).

§ γ. We have now given an outline of the ten arguments by which the Pyrrhonists attempted to demonstrate

[1] There are three kinds of relativity indicated in the ten τρόποι:
1st, The relation between object and subject;
2nd, The relation between object and object;
3rd, The relation between object and some pre-conceived maxim.
[2] *l. l.* 163.

the impossibility of determining the nature of the thing from the appearance, of the cause from the effect, the φαίνεσθαι ὄν from the φαίνεσθαι εἶναι..

These τρόποι are generally ascribed to Pyrrho himself, but by some authors to his admirer, Timon of Phlius. It is probable, however, that they are not the work of a single individual, but represent the accumulated reasonings of the Sceptics on the futility of sense-knowledge; and were collected by Sextus E., and inserted with regard to the following order[1]. The first four refer to simple perceptions, the next five to complex notions, the last to conventional ideas. This arrangement appears to be the same alluded to by Cicero: "Dividunt enim in partes, et eas quidem magnas: primum in sensus: deinde in ea, quæ ducuntur a sensibus, et ab omni consuetudine, quam obscurari volunt[2]." The first and fourth of the τρόποι, found upon the varying susceptibility of the percipient. Supposing there were constant and permanent causes in objects, our knowledge of them could never transcend their effects. But, since the operation of the *ego* as a concause introduces an element into the effect, variable and dependent upon the constitution of each individual, it follows that our knowledge of external things can amount to no more than a mere subjective

---

[1] For the order in which the τρόποι have been arranged by different writers, see Diogenes Laertius, ix. 87.

[2] Lucullus, 13. Compare also the threefold division of ideas in James Mill's *Analysis of the Mind*. "There are three classes of ideas, which we have occasion to name:

1st, Simple ideas, the copies of single sensations;

2nd, Complex ideas, copied directly from sensations;

3rd, Complex ideas, derived indeed from the senses, but put together in arbitrary combinations.

The two *former* may be called 'sensible,' the *last* 'mental' ideas."—Chap. IV. sec. I. p. 95. Aristoclus in Eus. *Præp. Ev.* speaks of the nine τρόποι of Ænesidemus; they were probably identical with the above, omitting the eighth, which is, in fact, only the expression of the conclusions from the others.

opinion or judgment. The ultra-materialist element observable in the theory of perception implied in these τρόποι, is of course not to be considered a feature of scepticism. The Sceptics particularly avoided positing any doctrine regarding the processes of cognition (λέγομεν καθ' οἷον δήποτε τρόπον· ἢ καθ' οἷον δήποτε τρόπον φαινομένων τε καὶ νοουμένων, ἵνα μὴ ζητᾶμεν πῶς φαίνεται τὰ φαινόμενα ἢ πῶς νοεῖται τὰ νοούμενα, ἀλλ' ἁπλῶς ταῦτα λαμβάνωμεν[1]).

The very nature of scepticism is to base its reasonings upon data furnished by positive and dogmatical systems of thought. Now the theory of knowledge upon which the Pyrrhonians proceeded was that of the Stoics. With them (the Stoics) mind was a mere material substance, a passive recipient of external impressions (ἀλλοιώσεις — τυπώσεις — φαντασίας).

No wonder then in the τρόποι we find the processes of perception not only compared to, but actually treated as analogous to, those of digestion. The mind is made to receive and assimilate its materials as the body its food, or as, the French Ideologists used to say, "the brain secretes thought as the liver secretes bile." We say then, in estimating the value of the sceptical arguments that we can only fairly consider them relatively to the data supplied by their opponents. Granting then that a mental image is scarcely more than the resultant of chemical[2] or even mechanical action, let us consider whether the Sceptics really handled the phenomena of perception in an accurate or philosophic manner, and whether they really succeeded in establishing a good case against the trustworthiness of the senses. Take, for example, the argument of the jaundiced or bloodshot eye.

[1] *Hyp.* I. 4. 9.
[2] "Plurima autem in illa tertia philosophiæ parte mutavit (sc. Zeno). In qua primum de sensibus ipsis quædam dixit nova, quos junctos esse censuit e quadam quasi impulsione oblata extrinsecus: quam ille φαντασίαν, nos *visum* appellemus."--*Ac. Post.* XI.

It is a capital instance with the Pyrrhonists, and is urged in reference to one or other of the senses in each of the ten τρόποι. In what does really the act of perception consist? Is it the absolute modification of consciousness? Is it not rather an apprehension of a succession of modifications? Sensitive perception (says Galen) consists not in the passive affection of the organ, but in the discriminative recognition —the dijudication of that affection by the active mind ("Εστι δὲ αἴσθησις οὐκ ἀλλοίωσις, ἀλλὰ διάγνωσις ἀλλοιώσεως¹). All the materialistic philosophers have concurred in this view. "To have no change of feeling is the same thing as to have no feeling at all. Sentire semper idem, et non sentire, ad idem recidunt²." The 'penser c'est sentir' school, indeed, denying any reflex operations to the mind, affirm that the knowledge of the change cannot be separated from the passive impression. "To have a different sensation, and to know that it is different, are not two things, but one and the same thing³." But still the essence of perception is discrimination. Where there is no power of discrimination there can be no perception properly so-called. Now the Pyrrhonists maintain that, because a white object appears yellow to a jaundiced eye, there is no credit to be placed in the reports of the senses. The fact is, to the jaundiced eye, not *only* white would appear yellow, but *every* other colour would be similarly modified⁴. Thus the discriminating faculty would be lost to the sense altogether, i.e.

---

[1] Galen, *de Placit. Hipp. et Plat.* LVII. cc. 14, 16, 17.
[2] Hobbes, *Elem. Philos.* P. IV. c. 25, § 5.
[3] James Mill, *On the Human Mind*, Vol. II. Sect. II.
[4] "Lurida præterea fiunt quæcumque tuentur
    Arquati, quia luroris de corpore eorum
    Semina multa fluunt simulacris obvia rerum,
    Multaque sunt oculis in eorum denique mixta
    Quæ contage sua palloribus omnia pingunt."
                               Lucretius, IV. 332—6.

there would be no perception through it. In point of fact people with blue eyes do not see everything blue, by virtue of the same dijudicative power. How few of those whose sense of hearing is otherwise acute are able to appreciate the distinctions of musical intervals. There must here be a defect, not in the sensorium but in the dijudicative faculty. Plato in the *Theætetus*, when confuting the doctrine Αἴσθησις = Ἐπιστήμη—shows that the knowledge we have of the objective and essential in things is obtained, not from any single perception, but from the judgments made by the mind through the comparison of several perceptions (ἀναλογιζομένη (ἡ ψυχὴ) ἐν ἑαυτῇ τὰ γεγονότα καὶ τὰ παρόντα πρὸς τὰ μέλλοντα[1]). This kind of knowledge corresponds to the ideas of reflection of Locke, the categories of Kant, or the relative suggestions of Brown, and is the condition of that comparing, abstracting, or generalising process, which is the foundation of all science. Now it is a question how far the validity of positive predication is open to the attacks of scepticism, when such predication is the consequence of purely mental comparisons. Mr Grote observes on this point, after commenting on that part of the discussion in the *Theætetus* which we have just noticed: "In the train of reasoning here terminated, Plato had been combating the doctrine Αἴσθησις = Ἐπιστήμη. In his sense of the word αἴσθησις he had refuted the doctrine. But what about the other doctrine, which he declares to be a part of the same programme—Homo Mensura—the Protagorean formula? That formula, so far from being refuted, is actually sustained and established by this train of reasoning. Plato has declared οὐσία, ἀλήθεια, ἐναντιότης, ἀγαθὸν, κακόν, etc. to be a distinct class of objects not perceived by sense. But he also tells us that they are apprehended by the mind through its own working, and that they are apprehended always in *relation to*

[1] *Theætetus*, 186 c.

each other. We *thus see that they are just as much relative* to *the concipient mind, as the objects of sense are to the percipient and sentient mind.* The *subject is the correlative limit or measure* (to use Protagorean phrases) *of one as well as of the other.* This confirms what I observed above, that the two doctrines, 1. Homo Mensura. 2. Αἴσθησις = Ἐπιστήμη—are completely distinct and independent, though Plato has chosen to implicate or identify them¹." Does then Mr Grote mean to assert that the relation discerned by the comparison of ideas is, in the same sense, relative to the comparing subject as the ideas themselves, considered as the simple products of sensible perception?—surely it is not so. In the *latter*, the terms related may be each unknown, and the resulting perception is but their ratio. In the *former*, however, these ratios are at least known as the terms of the new ratio which the mind evolves by its judging faculty. In the relativity of sensible perceptions are involved the physical conditions upon which our intercourse with the external world depends—but in mental judgments only the laws of thought or regulative principles of the understanding are operative. A sensible perception is a mere subjective accident, incapable of being expressed in language or made apprehensible to the consciousness of another, whereas mental conceptions are the contents of language and common to every one by whom the same language is spoken. Whether or not the Protagorean formula included any but mere external perceptions, it is at any rate certain that the ten τρόποι of the Pyrrhonists are only levelled against the products of sense, although they distinctly profess to be embodied by the Protagorean πρός τι—(πάλιν δὲ οἱ τρεῖς οὗτοι ἀνάγονται εἰς τὸ πρός τι· ὡς εἶναι γενικώτατον μὲν τὸν πρός τι, εἰδικοὺς δὲ τοὺς τρεῖς, ὑποβεβηκότας δὲ τοὺς δέκα²).

[1] Grote's *Plato*, Theætetus, Chap. xxvi. p. 373, Note *h*.
[2] *Hyp.* i. 13. 39.

We think[1] then that Plato was justified in identifying the Protagorean doctrine with that of knowledge being sensible perception, and that if this doctrine meant that each man is the measure of all things to himself, it never could have extended beyond that life of the individual which is made up of sense and memory. We nowhere find in ancient philosophy the distinction between the conceptive and imaginative faculties articulately enunciated, although to establish this distinction was probably the chief aim of the Platonic Psychology. The admission then of an idealistic theory of perception on the one hand, and the failure to distinguish clearly between the forms and materials of consciousness on the other, seem to have been the chief incentives to earlier Pyrrhonism. The Stoics, as we shall presently see, endeavoured to evade scepticism by substituting an ultra-realism for the idealism which prevailed to a greater or less degree among all the other sects of philosophers, and the adoption of Kantian principles, which clearly separate the thinking and imaginative faculties, preserves the modern Idealist from the paradoxes of the Sceptic. The burden then of meeting the Sceptical arguments rests with those who assert that the mind is only conscious of its own modifications, and that these modifications are but present or past sensations. In the *third* of the τρόποι seem to be suggested the germs of all those metaphysical theories respecting the relation between knowledge and existence, which, under one phrase or another, have occupied modern speculatists since the days of Descartes[2]. Into these questions it would be foreign to

[1] This opinion is at variance with that of the present standard authorities on the subject—Jowett, Grote, Dr Thompson. The discrepancy, I apprehend, arises from a difference in our point of view—epistemological or ontological.

[2] The reader will find every theory of Perception which has ever been propounded, named and classified by Sir William Hamilton in Note c. to his edition of Reid's *Works*.

our present purpose to enter, but we might remark that, to use a phrase common among philosophers of the present age, the problem involved is one which requires to be construed intelligibly to the mind, before it is worth while setting about the task of its solution. The two τρόποι most difficult to bring into the focus of modern intelligence are, perhaps, the second and tenth. In the second the feelings of pleasure and pain, which we rightly consider purely subjective[1] affections, are treated as being as much the immediate effects of external objective qualities in things, as the feeling of colour, heat, taste, etc. Thus, if A. and B. respectively like and dislike the same object, it is implied, that this discrepancy argues a difference in their perceptions of the same object, "τὸ δὲ διαφόροις χαίρειν τοῦ παρηλλαγμένας ἀπὸ τῶν ὑποκειμένων φαντασίας λαμβάνειν ἐστὶ μηνυτικόν[2]." To explicate this, we must again remind the reader that the Sceptics often made use of weapons placed in their hands by their adversaries. The Stoics held the doctrine that pleasure and pain were the forms under which men were affected by external objects in accordance with a fixed law of Nature; that that which was conformable to nature must produce pleasure, that which was contrary to it pain. Admitting the existence of such a law, then, it was competent to the Sceptics to argue that, since the discrepancy in the tastes of men was too proverbial to be called in question, this variety must arise from the *different*

---

[1] Man nennt aber die Fahigkeit, Lust oder Unlust, bei einer Vorstellung zu haben, darum Gefühl, weil beides das blos *Subjective* im Verhältnisse unserer Vorstellung, und gar keine Beziehung auf ein Object zum möglichen Erkenntnisse desselben (nicht einmal dem Erkenntnisse unseres Zustandes) enthält; da sonst selbst Empfindungen, ausser der Qualität, die ihnen der Beschaffenheit des *Subjects* wegen anhängt (z. B. des Rothen, des Süssen u.s.w.), doch auch als Erkenntniss-stücke auf ein *Object* bezogen werden, die Lust oder Unlust, aber (am Rothen und Süssen) schlechterdings nichts am Objecte, sondern lediglich Beziehung aufs Subject ausdrückt."—Kant's *Einleitung in die Metaphysik der Sitten,* i.

[2] *Hyp.* i. 14. 89.

mental representations which *different* individuals receive from the same object. For, as that which was agreeable to one person was so necessarily, and by nature, and as nature was uniform, it was impossible it could be disagreeable to another, unless through presenting a different appearance. "Non potest animal ullum non appetere id, quod accommodatum ad naturam appareat (Græci id οἰκεῖον appellant[1]." A similar explanation may be given of the tenth τρόπος, in which is contained the rather startling argumentation, *that* the want of uniformity in the laws, customs, and institutions among nations is an evidence of our inability to discover the real qualities of objects. Plutarch, however, affords us some means of detecting the drift of the sceptical reasoning. "῞Οτι μὲν γὰρ αἰσθητά ἐστι τἀγαθὰ καὶ τὰ κακὰ καὶ τούτοις ἐκποιεῖ λέγειν· οὐ γὰρ μόνον τὰ πάθη ἐστὶν αἰσθητὰ σὺν τοῖς εἴδεσιν, οἷον λύπη καὶ φόβος καὶ τὰ παραπλήσια, ἀλλὰ καὶ κλοπῆς καὶ μοιχείας καὶ τῶν ὁμοίων ἐστιν αἰσθέσθαι, καὶ καθόλου ἀφροσύνης καὶ δειλίας καὶ ἄλλων οὐκ ὀλίγων κακιῶν· οὐδὲ μόνον χαρᾶς καὶ εὐεργεσιῶν καὶ ἄλλων πολλῶν κατορθώσεων, ἀλλὰ φρονήσεως καὶ ἀνδρείας καὶ τῶν λοιπῶν ἀρετῶν[2]." From this passage it seems that the Stoics extended their theory about pleasure and pain to the apprehensions of good and evil, considering them to have arisen from sensible impressions, which obtain their distinctions under a ruling principle in nature, viz. the *summum bonum*. The Pyrrhonists therefore force their opponents into the dilemma, either of denying the existence of such an uniform law, or, from the fact of the conflicting ideas found to prevail about right and wrong, to be obliged to admit that perceptions could only be grounds of opinion, not of certainty. The Stoics, however, were at no loss to find an escape from the

[1] Lucullus, 12.
[2] Chrysipp. ap. *Plut. de Stoic. Rep.* 19.

difficulties in which their own principles involved them. They endeavoured to discover a criterion of truth, as a means of distinguishing true from false perceptions. But the discussion of this point would bring us into the midst of the polemic between the Sceptics and the Stoical dogmatists, a sketch of which we will present in the ensuing Lecture.

LECTURE IV.

ON THE PSYCHOLOGY OF THE STOICS.

"Les hommes cherchent ce qu'ils savent, et ne savent pas ce qu'ils cherchent."

§ α. THE Pyrrhonian philosophy had two developments, separated by a period of about 300 years. During the earlier period, Pyrrho himself promulgated his doctrines, which were not much more advanced than those we have discussed in the preceding Lecture. The moral element of his teaching, as we have already remarked, is scarcely discernible in any but the earliest form of the system. After the death of Timon of Phlius, friend and pupil of Pyrrho (who flourished about B.C. 272), little is known of Pyrrhonism, till it reappeared in a somewhat modified shape in the teachings of Ænesidemus and Agrippa, about the beginning of the Christian era. This later manifestation of scepticism we shall consider afterwards. It is our purpose in the present Lecture to follow the fortunes of Greek philosophy during the interval which elapsed between the age of Pyrrho and that of Ænesidemus. However great may have been the difference in the original views of Plato and Aristotle themselves, it seems that in the hands of their respective followers, viz. the Academics and Peripatetics, these were so far modified, that, according to Cicero, there ceased to be any perceptible difference between them: "Peripateticos et Academicos, nominibus differentes, re congruentes[1]." Their united forces, however, were apparently of little avail in opposing the advance of scepticism, whose positions, established and fortified by Pyrrho, were unassailable, either by the arguments of reason or the evidence of facts.

In truth, the Sceptics had so opposed φαινόμενα to νοούμενα, the reports of sense to the conclusions of reason, that their adversaries could hardly use one or the other, without laying themselves open to the possibility of being defeated with their own weapons. Did the dogmatists not say that truth originated in the senses, but that the power of judging of the truth was not in the senses? The intellect, they asserted, was the judge of things, and alone worthy of belief, because it alone discerned that which was simple and uniform, and perceived its real character: "Quanquam oriretur a sensibus, tamen non esse judicium veritatis in sensibus. Mentem volebant rerum esse judicem: solam censebant idoneam, cui crederetur; quia sola cerneret id, quod semper esset, simplex, et uniusmodi, et tale quale esset[2]." But, replied the Sceptic, if the senses are fallacious, where are the materials of reason? If they are true, what faith can be placed in the processes of the intellect? "Ergo si, rebus comprehensis et perceptis nisa et progressa ratio hoc efficiet, nihil posse comprehendi: quid potest reperiri, quod ipsum sibi repugnet magis[3]?" For have we not by those very processes proved, by a multitude of arguments, the falsity of the senses? If reason and common sense bear opposite testimony, who is to believe either, whether in the simple judgments that accompany recognition, or the artificial generalisations of your scientific method? εἰ γὰρ τοιοῦ-

---

[1] Lucullus, 5. [2] Ac. Post. 8. [3] Lucullus, 14.

IV.]   THE PSYCHOLOGY OF THE STOICS.   65

τος ἀπατεών ἐστιν ὁ λόγος, ὥστε καὶ τὰ φαινόμενα μονονουχὶ τῶν ὀφθαλμῶν ἡμῶν ὑφαρπάζειν, πῶς οὐ χρὴ ὑφορᾶσθαι αὐτὸν ἐν τοῖς ἀδήλοις ὥστε μὴ κατακολουθοῦντας αὐτῷ προπετεύεσθαι[1].

Thus Scepticism, like a spectral enemy, eluded every method of refutation, and by its presence seemed to threaten the existence of all science and certitude. An attempt, however, was made (with what success we shall see) to weaken the influence of scepticism, by a new school of philosophy, founded by Zeno of Cittium, which, taking its name from the Portico (στοά) at Athens, where their meetings were originally held, became known to the world as the celebrated sect of the Stoics. This school, the rise of which may be regarded as a direct effect of Pyrrhonism, united in its doctrines the scientific method of the Peripatetics, and the ascetic morality of the Cynics, with a theological pantheism[2] or hylozoism, and a psychological materialism peculiar to itself. Like Locke in the last century, Zeno thought that the best way of settling the controversies about the nature, extent, and certainty of human knowledge, was, to reconsider the whole subject; investigate the origin of all the materials of thought; and analyse, if possible, the operations of the mind in the acquisition and retention of its ideas and notions. We have seen that the favourite position of the Sceptics, and the one from which it was apparently the most difficult to dislodge them, was that of the co-operation in the production of ideas of the mind

[1] *Hyp.* I. 10, 20.
[2] "We do not deny it to be possible, but that some in all ages might have entertained such an atheistical conceit as this—that the original of this whole mundane system was from one artificial, orderly, and methodical, but senseless nature, lodged in the matter : but we cannot trace the footsteps of this doctrine anywhere so much as among the Stoics, to which sect Seneca, who speaks so waveringly and uncertainly on this point (whether the world were an animal or a plant), belonged."—Cudworth's *Intellectual System*, Vol. I. chap. III., XXVIII.

L. L.

itself, whose varying susceptibility renders the action of external causes so uncertain, that our knowledge of them can only be said to amount to an opinion. It was in direct opposition to this notion that Zeno enunciated two principles, which form the starting-point and basis of his whole psychological system: viz. 1st, the complete passivity of the mind under the influence of external objects; 2nd, the non-existence of any mind whatever prior to its reception of such external impressions. All nature, according to the Stoics, was the manifestation of one primordial substance, of which both the mind or soul of man and the external universe were but different modifications. "Statuebat enim ignem esse ipsam naturam, quæ quidque gigneret, et mentem atque sensus[1]." The soul of man consisted of eight parts, of which the principal was τὸ ἡγεμονικὸν or λόγισμος, the governing or reasoning faculty, and from this the senses took their origin. "When a man was born (said the Stoics) the ἡγεμονικὸν μέρος resembled a sheet of white paper (χαρτίον ἐνεργὸν εἰς ἀπογραφήν), and on this were to be stamped all the impressions received from external objects. The first characters it receives are those through the senses, for the mind having perceived anything, as, for example, a white object, bears away a remembrance of it when absent. After it has received and retained many like impressions, it is said to possess experience, for experience is a multitude of similar impressions (ἐμπειρία γάρ ἐστι τὸ τῶν ὁμοειδῶν φαντασιῶν πλῆθος). Of these presentations some are produced naturally (φυσικῶς) and undesignedly (ἀνεπιτεχνήτως), others we acquire through study and careful observation (δι' ἡμετέρας διδασκαλίας καὶ ἐπιμελείας). The *latter* are called ἔννοιαι, or *scientific ideas*, the *former* προλήψεις, or *simple ideas*. But reason (ὁ λόγος), in virtue of which we are called rational beings (λογικοί), is said to be developed in fourteen years

[1] *Acad. Post.* 11.

from natural and accidental ideas (προλήψεις). A rational being has also the capacity of forming a concept (νόημα), or idea of the understanding (φάντασμα διανοίας), and this faculty belongs to men and the gods alone[1]." In the account given above of the Stoical psychology, we see the origin of the well-known doctrine, which was afterwards adopted by Locke[2]: "Nihil in intellectu, quod non prius fuerit in sensu." But the Stoics gave a much wider significance to this principle, for they not only meant to imply that there *was* nothing in the mind which had not entered through the senses, but that there *could* be nothing in the mind which was not founded upon something existing in the real and external universe. It was by this, indeed, they hoped to turn the principal argument of the Sceptics, viz. the inability of reason to correct the mistakes of the senses. The mind, according to the description given in this passage from Plutarch, is built up through the aggregation[3] of ideas from without, προλήψεις—(ὁ δὲ λόγος, καθ' ὃν προσαγορευόμεθα λογικοί, ἐκ τῶν προλήψεων συμπληροῦσθαι λέγεται). Reason, in fact, seems to have been considered by the Stoics as little more than memory or experience, and since it was wholly composed of ideas whose archetypes were real and external objects, it followed that, being a storehouse of true impressions, a criterion might always be found in it, by

---

[1] Plutarch, *de Plac. Ph.* IV. 11.

[2] In regard to the passage (*De An.* L. III. c. 5) in which the intellect prior to experience is compared to a tablet on which nothing has actually been written, the context shows that the import of this simile is with Aristotle very different from what it is with the Stoics; to whom, it may be noticed, and not, as is usually supposed, to the Stagirite, are we to refer the first enouncement of the *brocard*—In Intellectu nihil est, quod non prius fuerit in Sensu. See Hamilton's Reid.

[3] It is not to be supposed that the κοιναὶ ἔννοιαι, φυσικαὶ προλήψεις, of the Stoics, far less of the Epicureans, were more than generalisations à *posteriori*. Yet this is a mistake into which, among many others, even Lipsius and Leibnitz have fallen.—Reid's *Works* (Hamilton), note A, page 774 (note).

which to test the validity of any new perception : "Quod autem erat sensu comprehensum, id ipsum *sensum* appellabat; et, si ita erat comprehensum, ut convelli ratione non posset, *scientiam:* sin aliter, *inscientiam* nominabat: ex qua exsisteret etiam *opinio,* quae esset imbecilla[1]." The faculties of the mind, according to the Stoics, were simply *sensation* and *memory,* and these are the only powers allowed it by the modern Materialists. It is true, Plutarch speaks of a general notion or conception, ἐννόημα, but this, he adds emphatically, is of the genus φάντασμα, i.e. it belonged to what we should call the imagination, and not the conceptive faculty[2] (ἔστι δὲ νόημα φάντασμα διανοίας λογικοῦ ζῴου· τὸ γὰρ φάντασμα, ἐπειδὰν λογικῇ προσπίπτῃ ψυχῇ, τότε ἐννόημα καλεῖται, εἰληφὸς τοὔνομα παρὰ τὸν νοῦν, διόπερ ὅσα τοῖς ἄλλοις ζῴοις προσπίπτει, ταῦτα φαντάσματα μόνον ἐστίν, ὅσα δὲ καὶ τοῖς θεοῖς καὶ τοῖς ἡμῖν γε, ταῦτα καὶ φαντάσματα κατὰ γένος καὶ ἐννοήματα κατ' εἶδος). This error, of classing general notions or conceptions with the mere sensible impressions of memory, an error which exposed Locke to so much ridicule from hostile critics, was particularly guarded against by Aristotle, who expressly states: "The same affection happens in thinking of anything as in drawing it, for though we do not require any particular size in drawing a triangle, nevertheless we do draw it of some definite magnitude; and we think in the same manner, even if we do not think it of *any* particular magnitude,—we place *some* magnitude before the eyes. If the thing itself is of an undefinable magnitude, we still imagine it of some definite magnitude[3]." The only way of

---

[1] *Acad. Post.* 11.
[2] For the distinction between Imagination and Conception, see Mansel's *Prolegomena Logica,* ch. I.
[3] "συμβαίνει γὰρ τὸ αὐτὸ πάθος ἐν τῷ νοεῖν ὅπερ καὶ ἐν τῷ διαγράφειν· ἐκεῖ τε γὰρ οὐθὲν προσχρώμενοι τῷ τὸ ποσὸν ὡρισμένον εἶναι τὸ τριγώνου, ὅμως γράφομεν ὡρισμένον κατὰ τὸ ποσόν· καὶ ὁ νοῶν ὡσαύτως, κἂν μὴ ποσὸν νοῇ, τίθεται πρὸ ὀμμάτων ποσόν, νοεῖ δ' οὐχ ᾗ ποσόν· ἂν δ' ἡ φύσις ᾗ τῶν ποσῶν,

escape for the Materialist is in ultra-nominalism, which allows the concept no existence in thought. But how did the Stoics, by reducing the mind to sensations and the memory of sensations, hope to further their object, viz. the establishment of some certain basis on which to build the truths of science and morals? The real problem Scepticism offered for solution was *this*, *When* we compare *objects* for the sake of observing their resemblance or difference, how do we know that the resemblances or differences we *think* we *perceive* are *intrinsically* in the *objects*, and do not arise from differences in the points of view under which we consider them, so that, in classifying or arranging, we are but classifying and arranging *appearances*, not *things?* It must be confessed the Stoics never met this question fairly. Ideas, they insisted, were the correlates of things, and he who discriminated ideas could discriminate things. "There is the greatest truth in the senses," says Antiochus, defending the Stoics, "if they are in sound and healthy order, and if everything is removed which could impede or hinder them— so that there is not one of us who in each one of his senses requires a more acute judgment as to each sort of thing." But, replies the Sceptic, what does this judgment amount to? You pronounce that an object is such and such, *because* the sensations you *receive* from it *now* are the *same* as, your memory tells you, you *derived* from it *before*. "So a skilled ear at the first note of a musical composition can say, that is the *Antiope* or the *Andromache*, when there are others, you admit, who have not even a suspicion of it[1]." Of course then on this point the judgment of the musician and the non-musician would be different. The fact alone would verify the truth or falsity of each. Now, continues the Sceptic,

ἀόριστον δέ, τίθεται μὲν ποσὸν ὡρισμένον, νοεῖ δ' ᾗ ποσὸν μόνον."—Aristotle (Περὶ Μνημῆς, κ.τ.λ.).
[1] Lucullus, 7; compare 27.

the *fact* may verify the *judgment*, but I want a judgment which can pronounce *à priori* on the fact. To this the Stoic replied, that the impressions of memory were the ultimate tests of truth, for memory had once been sensation, and the reality of its impressions would stand on the same footing as that of present perceptions. So Antiochus urges, if ἔννοιαι (notions) were false, or impressed from perceptions of such a kind as not to be able to be distinguished from false ones, then I should like to know how we were to use them, and how we were to see what was consistent with each thing, and what was inconsistent with it? Certainly no room is here left for memory, which alone contains not only philosophy, but the whole practice of life, and all the arts. For what memory can there be of what is false? or what does any one remember which he does not comprehend and hold in his mind? "Memoriæ quidem certe, quæ non modo philosophiam, sed omnis vitæ usum omnesque artes una maxime continet, nihil omnino loci relinquitur. Quæ potest enim esse memoria falsorum, aut quid quisquam meminit, quod non animo comprehendit et tenet[1]?"

In this passage is revealed at once both the strength and the weakness of the Stoical system. The strength, inasmuch as it furnishes a groundwork of common sense, and the universal belief of mankind, on which to found sufficient certitude for the requirements of life: on the other hand, the real question of knowledge, in the philosophical sense of the word, was abandoned. Knowledge here meant only recognition, and the ability to discriminate rightly, instead of being that *à priori* idea, by which we could pronounce what anything *is*, from the knowledge of what it *ought to be*. The reader of the *Theætetus* will readily discern the drift of this discussion; he will perceive that the knowledge which the Stoics professed to have of the external universe was limited

[1] Lucullus, 7.

to that faculty of right judgment which Plato there shows to be an inadequate notion of cognition (Λείπεται τοίνυν τὰ ψευδῆ δοξάσαι ἐν τῷδε, ὅταν γιγνώσκων σὲ καὶ Θεόδωρον καὶ ἔχων ἐν ἐκείνῳ τῷ κηρίνῳ ὥσπερ δακτυλίων σφῷν ἀμφοῖν τὰ σημεῖα, διὰ μακροῦ καὶ μὴ ἱκανῶς ὁρῶν ἄμφω, προθυμηθῶ, τὸ οἰκεῖον ἑκατέρου σημεῖον ἀποδοὺς τῇ οἰκείᾳ ὄψει, ἐμβιβάσας προσαρμόσαι εἰς τὸ ἑαυτῆς ἴχνος, ἵνα γένηται ἀναγνώρισις, εἶτα τούτων ἀποτυχὼν καὶ ὥσπερ οἱ ἔμπαλιν ὑποδούμενοι παραλλάξας προσβάλω τὴν ἑκατέρου ὄψιν πρὸς τὸ ἀλλότριον σημεῖον, ἢ καὶ, οἷα τὰ ἐν τοῖς κατόπτροις τῆς ὄψεως πάθη δεξιὰ εἰς ἀριστερὰ μεταρρεούσης, ταὐτὸν παθὼν διαμάρτω· τότε δὴ συμβαίνει ἡ ἑτεροδοξία καὶ τὸ ψευδῆ δοξάζειν)[1].

§ β. The cardinal notion of the Stoics is contained in the last clause of the paragraph we have quoted from Lucullus, in the preceding section, "quod non animo comprehendit." This comprehension (κατάληψις), which we think we shall be able to show was little more than the "involuntary association" of the modern Materialists[2], was defined by the Stoics as the instinctive discrimination of the mind between real and false impressions. "For," said they, "we ought not to give credit to everything which is perceived, but only to those perceptions which contain some especial mark of those things which appeared[3]." Such a perception then was called the cataleptic phantasm (φαντασία καταληπτική), or comprehensible perception. As this cataleptic phantasm was the grand *crux* or bone of contention between the Stoics and New Academy, during a succession of generations, and as it illustrates the chief peculiarity of the dogmatic empiricism which was the only positive system of philosophy then prevalent in Greece, we shall endeavour to explicate its real

[1] *Theætetus*, 193, b. c.
[2] The reader will remember Hume's notion of belief. The subject is clearly expounded in the chapter "On Belief" in the *Analysis of the Human Mind*, by James Mill (Vol. I. c. XI.).
[3] *Acad. Post.* 11.

meaning. Philosophers had discovered in man the faculty of abstracting in perception the *phenomenal appearance* from the *objective reality*. The Stoics were the first to attempt to bridge over this gulf between the *object* in *thought* and the *object* in *nature*, τὰ ἡμῖν and τὰ φύσει. They maintained that this object of thought was co-extensive with the real object, that *although* with reference to the mind it was an image, or, as Chrysippus thought, a modification (ἀλλοίωσις), *still* it covered, embraced, and comprehended the object, so that the perception was in fact intuitive, and our knowledge was not that of the mere *subject-object*, but of the *object-object*. φαντασία δὲ τύπωσις ἐν ψυχῇ, τουτέστιν ἀλλοίωσις. οὐ γὰρ δεκτέον τὴν τύπωσιν, οἱονεὶ τύπον σφραγιστῆρος· ἐπεὶ ἀνένδεκτόν ἐστι πολλοὺς τύπους κατὰ τὸ αὐτὸ περιγίνεσθαι. νοεῖται δὲ φαντασία ἡ ἀπὸ ὑπάρχοντος κατὰ τὸ ὑπάρχον ἐναπομεμαγμένη καὶ ἐναποτετυπωμένη καὶ ἐναποσφραγισμένη, οἵα οὐκ ἂν γένοιτο ἀπὸ μὴ ὑπάρχοντος[1]. Besides this theory of the relation of knowledge to existence, the Stoics also thought that every object had by nature a distinctive or characteristic mark, so that there were not two objects, however similar in appearance, which really were identical on close inspection. "Omnia dicis sui generis esse; nihil esse idem, quod sit aliud. Stoicum est quidem, nec admodum incredibile; nullum esse pilum omnibus rebus talem, qualis sit pilus alius nullum gramen[2]." It is in connexion with these two notions that we must look for an explanation of the cataleptic phantasm. Since perception was an intuition of a real external object, and no two objects in nature were exactly alike, it was possible for a

---

[1] Diogenes Laertius, Lib. VII. cap. I. 50.
Cf. "The external senses have a double province—to make us feel, and to make us perceive. They furnish us with a variety of sensations—some pleasant, others painful, and others indifferent; at the same time, they give us a conception and an invincible belief of the existence of external objects."
—Reid, *On the Int. Powers*, Essay II. c. XVII. p. 318.

[2] Lucullus, 26.

wise man to discern this mark or distinctive feature of objects, and, by storing it up in the memory, make it a criterion with which to compare other perceptions or observations[1]. Thus Epicurus, identifying πρόληψις with κατάληψις, says it is a

[1] The student will find that the dispute between the Stoics and Academicians was not *really* about objective ontological existence, but an enquiry into the nature of evidence as a ground of inference. The same point is elucidated by Mr Mill in his *Logic*, Book IV. ch. I. § 2: "In almost every act of our perceiving faculties, observation and inference are intimately blended. What we are said to observe is usually a compound result, of which one-tenth may be observation, and the remaining nine-tenths inference. I affirm, for example, that I hear a man's voice. This would pass, in common language, for a direct perception. All, however, which is really perception is that I hear a sound. That the sound is a voice, and that voice the voice of a man, are not perceptions, but inferences. I affirm, again, that I saw my brother at a certain hour this morning. If any proposition concerning a matter of fact would commonly be said to be known by the direct testimony of the senses, this surely would be so. The truth, however, is far otherwise. I only saw a certain coloured surface; or, rather, I had the kind of visual sensations which are usually produced by a coloured surface; and from these as marks, known to be such by previous experience, I concluded I saw my brother. I might have had sensations precisely similar when my brother was not there. I might have seen some other person so nearly resembling him in appearance, as, at the distance, and with the degree of attention which I bestowed, to be mistaken for him. I might have been asleep, and have dreamed that I saw him, or in a state of nervous disorder which brought his image before me in a waking hallucination. In all these modes, many have been led to believe that they saw persons well known to them, who were dead, or far distant. If any of these suppositions had been true, the affirmation, that I saw my brother, would have been erroneous, but whatever was matter of direct perception, namely, the visual sensations, would have been real. The inference only would have been ill-grounded; I should have ascribed those sensations to a wrong cause."

The reasoning runs thus: such and such marks are marks of my brother, here are such and such marks, therefore here is my brother. But in the major proposition the induction does not preclude the possibility of a plurality of causes. Such and such marks may belong to other people besides my brother, hence the Stoical assumption, that everything had a distinctive mark. The reader will find the whole of the *Lucullus* turns upon the above passage from Mr Mill. The reason why the ontological and logical notions were confounded arose from the misapprehension as to the nature of the copula which was supposed to import real existence.

See in the ensuing Lecture the account of the doctrine of *probability* of Carneades.

right opinion, notion, or general idea in the mind, i.e. a remembrance of things which have often appeared externally (Ἐπίκουρος δὲ ὁ φιλόσοφος λέγει πρόληψιν οἱονεὶ κατάληψιν, ἢ δόξαν ὀρθήν, ἢ ἔννοιαν, ἢ καθολικὴν νόησιν ἐναποκειμένην, τουτέστι μνήμην τοῦ πολλάκις ἔξωθεν φανέντος[1]). It is probable that the cataleptic phantasm was really a complex idea[2] in memory, composed of a group of those marks or qualities which constitute the differentia of a species. Thus Zeno, comparing the steps of the process by which the mind acquires its furniture, to the open palm, the half-closed hand, the closed fist, and that again grasped by the other hand, illustrated the method of arriving at science or knowledge by observation, comparison, abstraction, and classification; but of course, if the mind could grasp single objects so as to recognise them by their accidents, *à fortiori* it could acquire those complex conceptions through which we refer an individual to its species. So the cataleptic phantasm seems to be, sometimes a single complex perception of an individual, and sometimes a more general notion. Cicero appears, however, to regard it always as the former, although the basis on which the validity of general notions was established. " Quodque natura quasi normam scientiæ et principium sui dedisset, unde postea notiones rerum in animis imprimerentur; e quibus non principium solum, sed latiores quædam, ad rationem inveniendam viæ reperiuntur[3]."

§ γ. We have before remarked that the passivity of the mind in perception was one of the most prominent features in the Stoical system. The assent (συγκατάθεσις) with which the mind accepted phenomena was involuntary, and it is not

[1] Suidas in πρόληψις.
[2] Compare the description of a Conception in James Mill: "My *conception* of a horse is merely my taking together, in one, the simple ideas of the sensations which constitute my knowledge of a horse."—*Analysis of the Human Mind*, Vol. I. chap. vi. p. 175.
[3] *Acad. Post.* 11.

very easy to see in this respect how the Stoical notion of knowledge was so very different from that of opinion or simple judgment, between which extremes comprehension or κατάληψις occupied the middle place. According to Gellius, assent was *voluntary*, and in this *knowledge* differed from *opinion*, the latter being *involuntary* and receiving no assent from the mind. "Visa animi, quas φαντασίας philosophi appellant, quibus mens hominis prima statim specie accidentis rei pellitur, non voluntatis sunt neque arbitraria, sed vi quadam sua inferunt sese hominibus noscitanda. Probationes autem, quas συγκαταθέσεις vocant, quibus eadem visa noscuntur ac dijudicantur, voluntaria sunt fiuntque hominum arbitratu[1]." On the other hand, Cicero, discussing the same subject, seems to leave the voluntariness of assent as very doubtful. "For as it is evident (says Lucullus) that one scale of a balance must be depressed when a weight is put in it, so the mind too must yield to what is evident; for just as it is impossible for any animal to forbear desiring what is manifestly suited to its nature, so it is equally impossible for it to withhold its assent to a manifest fact which is brought under its notice[2]." To reconcile these conflicting statements we must have recourse to the physical theory of the Stoics, which powerfully influenced the logic as well as the ethic of their whole system. They thought that "the whole universe being material, there was a reason immanent in everything, under the fixed and immutable laws of which all nature developed after its kind." But to avoid the fatalism which such a principle would involve, Chrysippus insisted on the doctrine of "auxiliary causes," or confatalism, by which, although the action of

---

[1] Gellius, xix. cap. i. It is probable that the act of inference was the voluntary part of the process of knowledge; simple judgment was involuntary; but inference involves the weighing of evidence, hence the simile above from Lucullus.—See Note 17, from Mill's *Logic*.
[2] Lucullus, 12.

nature was fixed, *still*, as every event was the resultant of compounded causes, so their concomitance as a condition of the coefficiency of each cause was contingent. For example, motion must ensue to a body on the application of a force. But the same force might communicate a motion of rotation to *one* body, and a motion of translation to *another*. Thus (says Chrysippus) "a man who pushes a cylinder gives it a principle of motion, but not immediately that of revolution. So, an object strikes our sense and conveys its image to our soul, yet leaves us free to believe in it or not; as in the case of the cylinder which is set in motion from without, it will continue for the future to move according to its own proper force and nature." "Ut igitur, inquit, qui protrusit cylindrum, dedit ei principium motionis, volubilitatem autem non dedit: sic visum objectum imprimit illud quidem, et quasi signabit in animo suam speciem: sed assensio nostra erit in potestate: eaque quemadmodum in cylindro dictum est, extrinsecus pulsa, quod reliquum est suapte vi et natura movebitur[1]." Still, this belief or assent of the mind was the result of the action of an immutable law, and therefore, as is the inevitable consequence of materialistic principles, the pure spontaneity of the mind is not admitted. It is true it acts according to its own nature, and so far as its action is a concause its determination is voluntary. What was this law under which the mind evolved its knowledge? Modern philosophers would call it the law of "the association of ideas," the principle under which belief and knowledge are alike involuntary. The *first* law, property, or faculty of the human mind brought into operation in earliest infancy is that of the association of ideas. To recollect, to imagine, to abstract, and to reason, according to the Hume, Brown, and Mill school of philosophy, are not *active*, but *neuter* verbs, implying a succession of mental states, determined by this fixed

[1] *De Fato*, 19.

law of association and suggestion, of which the mind is the passive subject[1]. Ancient Philosophy, however, was not ripe for such an articulate enunciation of the views which they yet unconsciously foreshadowed, the complete systematization of which was reserved for the philosophers of the eighteenth century[2].

§ 5. In the complete antithesis the Stoics intended their system to exhibit to the pernicious opinions of the

---

[1] Brown's celebrated analysis of the process of composition is a luminous illustration of this theory:—" In the first place, to sit down to compose, is to have a general notion of some subject which we are about to treat, with the desire of developing it, and the expectation, or perhaps the confidence, that we shall be able to develop it more or less fully. The desire, like every other vivid feeling, has a degree of permanence which our vivid feelings only possess; and, by its permanence, tends to keep the accompanying conception of the subject, which is the object of the desire, also permanent before us; and while it is thus permanent the usual spontaneous suggestions take place—conception following conception, in rapid but relative series, and our judgment, all the time, approving and rejecting, according to those relations of fitness and unfitness to the subject, which it perceives in the parts of the train. Such I conceive to be a faithful picture of the state, or successive states of the mind, in the process of composition. It is not the exercise of a single power, but the development of various susceptibilities—of desire—of simple suggestion, by which conceptions rise after conceptions—of judgment, or relative suggestion, by which a feeling of relative fitness or unfitness arises, on the contemplation of the conceptions that have thus spontaneously presented themselves. We think of some subject; the thought of this subject induces various conceptions related to it. We approve of some, as having a relation of fitness for our end, and disapprove of others, as unfit. We may term this complex state, or series of states, 'imagination,' or 'fancy,' and the term may be convenient for its brevity. But, in using it, we must not forget that the term, however brief and simple, is still the name of a state that is complex, or of a succession of certain states; that the phenomena comprehended under it, being the same in nature, are not rendered, by this use of a mere word, different from those to which we have already given peculiar names, expressive of them as they exist separately; and that it is to the classes of these elementary phenomena, therefore, that we must refer the whole process of imagination in our philosophic analysis—unless we exclude analysis altogether, and fill our mental vocabulary with as many names of powers as there are complex affections of the mind."—Dr Brown's *Lectures*. Lecture XLII. page 271.

[2] Hamilton's Reid. See notes to chap. VI. *On the Active Powers*, page 616.

Pyrrhonists, not only did they maintain that all sceptical doubt was inconsistent with knowledge, but also that all reasonable belief was insufficient for a wise man. "Mihi porro non tam certum est, esse aliquid, quod comprehendi possit, de quo jam nimium etiam diu disputo, quam sapientem nihil opinari, id est, nunquam assentire rei vel falsæ, vel incognitæ[1]," was a sentiment the Stoics were never tired of reiterating. Ignorance, opinion, and belief, were, with them, convertible terms, which might suffice for the unthinking, uneducated, and superstitious vulgar; but certainty, knowledge, and assent, were alone conformable to the wisdom of the thoughtful philosophic sage. It was this arrogation of absolute certainty, this dogmatic assumption of unqualified conviction, which, probably, first aroused the opposition of the successors of Plato in the Academy to the Stoical doctrines. Men who had read and understood the purport of the *Theætetus*, and who had in that work seen every empirical avenue to knowledge tested and found inadequate, whether it was sensation, judgment, or reason—men who had inherited and secretly cherished the belief of their immortal founder in the existence of principles in the higher reason of man, through which they had cognition of things prior to and beyond experience—these men would ill brook the usurpation of absolute knowledge, and certitude, by a set of philosophers who maintained that man was endowed with a soul which, previously to its contact with external phenomena, was devoid of every intellectual or moral attribute. It was probably, we say, such latent influences as these which tended to maintain that long hostility between the Stoics and later Academicians —an hostility which, although ostensibly confined to controversies respecting questions of apparently limited scope, yet involved problems of vital importance to the interests of moral and metaphysical truth.

[1] Lucullus, 18.

LECTURE V.

THE NEW ACADEMY.

"Εἰ μὴ γὰρ ἦν Χρύσιππος, οὐκ ἂν ἦν ἐγώ."

§ *a.* "HISTORIANS," says Sextus, "generally distinguish three Academies. A first and principal, founded by Plato himself; a second or middle, commencing with Arcesilas; a third or new, under the presidency of Carneades."

To these some writers add a fourth, under Philo and Charmidas, and even a fifth, that of Antiochus[1].

Cicero, however, seems to think, that if there ever was any divergence in the doctrines of the successors of Plato from the original method of their founder, it commenced with Arcesilas, who thus gave the distinguishing character to the New Academy: "Sed tamen illa, quam exposui, vetus; hæc nova nominetur: quæ usque ad Carneadem perducta, qui quartus ab Arcesila fuit, in eadem Arcesilæ ratione permansit[2]." Of the opinions of Arcesilas himself, however, we have not any very certain information; he appears to have appropriated so much of the scepticism of Pyrrho as was not inconsistent with the traditions of the Academy. But that

[1] *Hyp.* I. 33. 220. Eusebius, 14. 4. *Præparat. Evang.* p. 726.
[2] *Ac. Post.* 12. *De Fin.* v. 3.

by which he may be considered to have most especially determined the attitude of the Academy towards the Stoical dogmatists, was the controversy he commenced respecting the cataleptic phantasm, upon the validity of which, as a basis of certitude in the acquisition of knowledge, depended the pretensions of empiricism. This controversy lasted for nearly 300 years[1], according to the testimony of Cicero; and in fact has been, and for ever must be, the fundamental problem of metaphysics. If we have no knowledge prior to experience, *what degree* of certainty attached to the knowledge obtained from experience? *what* is the nature of that knowledge, and *what* its *extent?* After the lapse of so many centuries these questions seem as far from a satisfactory solution as ever. Perhaps, however, as Professor Ferrier remarks, that ever-increasing tendency among speculatists towards "the great gulf-stream of idealism" had already set in, being either the natural reaction from the materialistic realism of the Stoics, or a less positive form of the Platonic system. Both these influences are discernible in the opinions of Arcesilas, Carneades, and Philo. Idealism, however, was most articulately expressed by Carneades; and it is the dogmatic enunciation of the impotency of human knowledge to transcend the sphere of subjective reality, the ἀκατάληπτον, or incomprehensibility of all things, as it was then termed, which marks his speculations as the commencement of a new era in metaphysical philosophy, and, from their coincidence with the tendencies of thought of the present age, renders their explication at once easier and more interesting.

It is curious, indeed, to observe, how principles, the antithesis of which was as decided in the theories of Chrysippus and Carneades as in the corresponding speculative systems of the present day, should have led to results almost the opposite to those we are accustomed to consider as inevitable

[1] Lucullus, 24, et *passim*.

consequences from their respective premises. In Stoicism we have united a psychological system of materialism which left the human soul little better than an ingenious mechanism, a rigid morality whose precepts inculcated habits of fortitude and temperance, and a notion of causality which excluded all spontaneity from the voluntary effort, as well as from the cognitive process. On the other side, we have the absolute freedom of the active principle maintained by Carneades, side by side with total scepticism as to the existence of any motive to virtue beyond utility, and a denial of all external and objective elements in the materials of consciousness. But there is no doubt the Stoical doctrines, by reason of their scientific method, their elevated morality, and their accordance with the prevailing superstitions of the age, were much more popular among all who upheld the interests of religion and virtue, than the apparently lax scepticism of the New Academicians.

§ β. Carneades is certainly the representative man of the New Academy; and in his method and opinions we shall find the indications of that mighty change which was shortly to dislodge all the old-world notions so strenuously upheld and cherished by the Stoics: notions which, rooted in the pride of the reason of the learned, and in the traditional superstitions of the vulgar, it seemed the mission of Carneades and the later Academicians systematically to oppose. In truth the Stoics may be considered to have combined in their system all that was positive in theology, morality, and speculative science. Carneades, on the other hand, principally comes before us as embodying in his opinions the negation of every article of Stoicism; and it is this aspect, therefore, of his doctrines that we shall proceed to examine. Carneades, like most of the later Academicians, left no writings of his own; we have to seek for his views in the works of his illustrious expounder Cicero, who himself was perhaps the noblest upholder of the New Academy, and in those of Sextus Empiricus, whose scepticism perhaps leant more to that of Carneades than to that of Pyrrho. It is easy to detect, even from the brief sketch we have given of the Stoical doctrines, that their main positions may be reduced to *four* coherent and dependent articles; and it is with reference to each of these that we shall consider the opposing opinions of Carneades.

1. Their physical theory of the universe, as the inalienable and immortal subject of a one primary law or cause, which as a regulative, and by the Stoics considered an intelligent principle, determines and directs all the manifestations of nature. "Ait enim (sc. Chrysippus), vim divinam in ratione esse positam, et universæ naturæ animo atque mente: ipsumque mundum dicit esse, et ejus animi fusionem universam[1]."

2. That, under this law, cause, or principle, the successions and changes of things are the immutable links in an eternal sequence of causation ($εἱμαρμένη$), the passive involuntary agents of absolute necessity ("tum ejus ipsius principatum, qui in mente et ratione versetur, communemque rerum naturam, universa atque omnia continentem: tum fatalem vim, et necessitatem rerum futurarum)[2]."

3. That in the act of perception the mind or human subject is passively illuminated with a consciousness of its own existence, and that of the object causing the perception; and that this consciousness or cataleptic phantasm imparts the conviction of its own reality, conformity, and individuality "si illud esset (sc. $καταληπτικὴ$ $φαντασία$) sicut Zeno definiret, tale visum igitur impressum effictumque ex

---

[1] *De Nat. Deor.* I. 15.

[2] *l. l.* 15. "Hinc vobis exstitit primum illa fatalis necessitas, quam $εἱμαρμένην$ dicitis; ut, quidquid accidat, id ex æterna veritate, causarumque continuatione fluxisse dicatis."—*l. l.* 20.

eo, unde esset, quale esse non posset, ex eo, unde non esset¹."

4. That since knowledge is but the instinctive apprehension of the mind's obedience to the laws of its nature, it is not competent to a wise man to credit any authority or evidence short of this necessary assent which consciousness accords to the cataleptic phantasm (αὕτη γὰρ ἦν φασι κατάληψιν καὶ καταληπτικῆς φαντασίας συγκατάθεσιν ἤτοι ἐν σοφῷ ἢ ἐν φαύλῳ γίνεται. ἀλλ' ἐάν τε ἐν σοφῷ γένηται ἐπιστήμη ἐστίν, ἐάν τε ἐν φαύλῳ, δόξα)².

§ γ. To the first of these articles, embracing as it does the entire theology of the Stoics, Carneades opposed a multitude of arguments, which Cicero, in his treatise *De Natura Deorum*, has put into the mouth of Cotta, who speaks against the Epicureans as well as the Stoics. For although Cicero does not expressly attribute all the negative opinions in this work to Carneades, yet it is evident, from the identity of style between the reasonings of Cotta and those ascribed by name to Carneades, that they are the utterances of one mind; and especially from the exordium prefixed to the work we are led to the conclusion that they must have been eminently the sentiments of Carneades. "Contra quos (sc. Stoicos) Carneades ita multa disseruit, ut excitaret homines non socordes ad veri investigandi cupiditatem³."

The first book of this work is devoted to a controversy between C. Velleius on behalf of the Epicureans against Q. Lucilius Balbus defending the Stoics. In the second book the latter takes up the argument, and expounds and defends the theology of the Stoics; and in the third book Balbus is in turn attacked by Cotta as the representative of the New Academy.

"My belief in the existence of the gods," says Cotta,

¹ Lucullus, 6.   ² *Adv. Math.* VII. 153.
³ *De Nat. Deor.* I. 2.

"is based on the traditions of my ancestors; but since you disregard authorities, and appeal to reason, permit me to measure my reason against yours; for the proofs on which you found the existence of the gods tend only to render a proposition doubtful that in my opinion is not so." ("Affers haec omnia argumenta, cur dii sint: remque meâ sententiâ minime dubiam, argumentando dubiam facis[1].") This passage is remarkable as evincing the tremendous strides scepticism must have made in subverting the natural tendency of man to trust in the conclusions of his reason. That which is solely upheld by reason, the same reason may confute; but there *is* a belief not founded on demonstrative evidence which reason cannot touch. We see the traditional manner of the Old Academy preserved in the playful Socratic banter with which frequently the gravest subjects are handled; and highly characteristic of the contempt in which the logic of the Stoics was held by Carneades and his followers is the ensuing passage: "All that you have so much enlarged upon in treating this subject," observes Cotta, "is that old, concise, and, as it seemed to you, acute syllogism of Zeno, Quod ratione utitur, melius est, quam id, quod ratione non utitur. Nihil autem mundo melius. Ratione igitur mundus utitur[2]." By parity of reasoning Zeno could just as well prove that the world could read a book, for "that which can read is better than that which cannot;—nothing is better than the world, the world therefore can read. So arguing one might shew the world to be an orator, a mathematician, a musician,—that it professes all sciences, and in short is a philosopher." This is a good specimen of the mode of fence so often adopted by Carneades, which Cicero elsewhere tells us was particularly obnoxious to Chrysippus, his Stoical adversary. "Placet enim Chrysippo, cum gradatim interro-

---

[1] *De Nat. Deor.* III. 4. [2] *l. l.* 9.

getur, verbi causa, tria, pauca sint, anne multa: aliquanto prius, quam ad multa perveniat, quiescere, id est, quod ab iis dicitur, ἡσυχάζειν. Per me vel stertas licet, inquit Carneades, non modo quiescas. Sed quid proficit? sequitur enim qui te ex somno excitet, et eodem modo interroget[1]." If however the manner of Carneades was somewhat flippant, his arguments seem often to have been urged with great subtlety and acuteness. The reason or intelligence said to pervade nature by the Stoics, although considered by them an *efficient*, was really nothing more than a *physical cause*, the *natura naturans* of the Pantheist. When Cotta therefore distinguishes it from a *natural cause*, he apparently only means that the all-pervading law of the Stoics implies an unity, and in that sense a personality for the Deity, which the Academicians were not disposed to admit, although they allowed that the harmony and the regularity of the universe indicated the action of at least mechanical or perhaps chemical laws. "Itaque illa mihi placebat oratio de convenientia, consensuque naturæ, quam quasi cognatione continuatam conspirare dicebas. Illud non probabam, quod negabas id accidere potuisse, nisi ea uno divino spiritu contineretur. Illa vero cohæret et permanet, naturæ viribus, non deorum: estque in ea iste quasi consensus, quam συμπάθειαν Graeci vocant. Sed ea, quo sua sponte major est, eo minus divina ratione existimanda est[2]." In this however there is little more than a logical distinction. The *natura naturata* is but the passive subject, in which inheres the *natura naturans*, active in nothing but its logical antecedence[3]. Thus the broad distinction between the theological system of the

---

[1] Lucullus, 29.   [2] *De Nat. Deor.* III. 11.

[3] "Stoici naturam dividunt in duas partes: unam, quæ efficiat, alteram, quæ se ad faciendum tractabilem præstet. In illa prima esse vim faciendi, in hac materiam, nec alterum sine altero esse posse. Ita isti uno naturæ nomine res diversissimas comprehenderunt, Deum et mundum, artificem et opus, dicuntque, alterum sine altero, nihil posse, tamquam natura sit Deus

Epicureans and Academicians and that of the Stoics was, that while the *latter* conceived that passive matter could be endowed with a self-acting energy, the *former* saw that the forces and powers in nature were but attributes or properties of the material substance; and therefore merely physical laws, and not intelligent or efficient causes. The great incentive to Pantheism in all ages has been the inability of the human mind to conceive a *first* cause; a *primary* consequent which itself has had no antecedent. To avoid this the Pantheist devises the hypothesis of an eternal substance in which cause and effect are as it were synchronous.

There was no universe without a God, and no God independent of the universe. The notion of the immortality and the infinity of the material universe was an assumption essentially involved in the Pantheistic system, since it was absurd to suppose that *that*, the duration of which had been unlimited in the past, could terminate in any period of the future; and, as we have seen, this past eternity was the fundamental principle of the system. To demonstrate therefore the mortality, mutability, and finite nature of matter, would be to aim a fatal blow at the leading conception of the Pantheist. Cicero has preserved to us the argumentation of Carneades on the subject. The general scope of his reasoning seems to be that the attributes of a thing cannot be in their nature contrary to its essence; and that matter, as manifested to us, is mutable, soluble, and finite, *therefore* it is impossible to conceive it the inalienable seat of an immutable, immortal and infinite essence.

"Si nullum corpus immortale sit, nullum esse corpus sempiternum. Corpus autem immortale nullum esse, ne individuum quidem, nec quod dirimi, distrahive non possit. Cum-

mundo permistus, Nam interdum sic confundunt, ut sit Deus ipsa mens mundi, et mundus corpus Dei."—Lactantius, *Divinar. Instit.* lib. VII. cap. 3, p. 781.

que omne animal patibilem naturam habeat, nullum est eorum quod effugiat accipiendi aliquid extrinsecus, id est, quasi ferendi et patiendi necessitatem. Et, si omne animal mortale est, immortale nullum est. Ergo itidem si omne animal secari ac dividi potest, nullum est eorum individuum, nullum æternum. Atqui omne animal ad accipiendam vim externam, et ferendam paratum est. Mortale igitur omne animal, et dissolubile, et dividuum sit necesse est." (And again continues Carneades), "Si omnia, quæ sunt, e quibus cuncta constant, mutabilia sunt; nullum corpus esse potest non mutabile. Mutabilia autem sunt illa, ex quibus omnia constant, ut vobis videtur. Omne igitur corpus mutabile est. At si esset corpus aliquod immortale, non esset omne mutabile. Ita efficitur, ut omne corpus mortale sit.......Quod si ea intereant, ex quibus constet omne animal; nullum est animal sempiternum[1]." In all the above we see the same idea preserved, viz. that of the *passivity* of matter as contrasted with the *activity* of intelligence, which the Stoics consistently confounded, *both* in the reason of man as an individual, and in that of the universe as a whole. In fact, between a passive, suffering, perishable subject, and an active, efficient agent there is an entire diameter of being, which seems to separate them even in conception as much as in reality. Bishop Butler uses similar arguments to prove the immortality of the soul as Carneades to demonstrate the mortality of the universe, both endeavouring to show that a thinking principle, as in its essence *one* and *indivisible*, cannot be a function of that which is subject to perpetual flux and attrition. Carneades further indicates how the Pantheism of the Stoics leads to Polytheism, and hence to Fetishism.

For with the vulgar, to whom the metaphysic of the system would be unintelligible, the deification of the uni-

[1] *De Nat. Deor.* III. 12.

verse, by an easy transition, would be transferred to its parts;—so, "There is a divinity presiding over every human affair, and every idle phantasm, every figment of the imagination, are Deities." ("Ergo etiam Spes, Moneta omniaque, quæ cogitatione nobismet ipsis possumus fingere[1].") But enough has been said to prove the decided hostility of Carneades and the later Academicians to the theological doctrines of the Stoics, or, more properly, of the great mass of the heathen public. Ought Carneades then to be considered an atheist? Cicero denies that such a consequence would be consistent with any form of philosophy. "Hæc Carneades agebat; non ut deos tolleret; quid enim philosopho minus conveniens? sed ut Stoicos nihil de diis explicare convinceret[2]." Perhaps the divinity of the Academicians was that "*Unknown God*," whom St Paul told the Athenians, that having ignorantly worshipped he now declared unto them, (Ἐν αὐτῷ γὰρ ζῶμεν καὶ κινούμεθα καί ἐσμεν).

§ δ. The notion of a fatal necessity ordering and compelling both the actions of men, and the changes in the external universe, seems to have been ingrained in the Greek mind. Every poet, every tragedian, finds in this instinct a ready fountain of sympathy with his narrations, representing man as the sport of a relentless destiny, whose decrees he unconsciously fulfils, and yet is punished for obeying. This idea then, although common to the vulgar, and inextricably bound up with the ancient theogony of Greece, was really the logical consequence of a philosophical Pantheism. For it is impossible to conceive of law inherent in passive matter apart from an immutable order of succession—a chain every link of which is potentially involved in the primary principle. Such a result, however, when combined with psychological materialism, must evidently

---

[1] l. l. 18.   [2] l. l. 17.

lead to the denial of all freedom of will to the human agent.

This consequence, besides being opposed to the evidence of facts, would annihilate all moral responsibility, and therefore all distinctions between virtue and vice.

Thus ensued ample materials for the controversial propensities of the Stoics and their contemporaries; and their discussions, we are told, were dependent on three propositions, known among logicians as "*the dominative argument*," viz.

1. Πᾶν παρεληλυθὸς ἀληθὲς ἀναγκαῖον εἶναι.
2. Δυνατῷ ἀδύνατον μὴ ἀκολουθεῖν.
3. Δύνατον εἶναι ὃ οὔτ᾽ ἔστιν ἀληθὲς οὔτ᾽ ἔσται.

From the acceptance of any two of these propositions *followed* logically the *denial* of the *third*; and so the question of necessity or freedom in the succession of human events was supposed to be decided. The second or middle of these propositions was the most important, and may be thus interpreted: "All nature *either* acts in conformity to a fixed immutable law, or it *does not;* and it is impossible to conceive that the *same* law can be at one time *fixed* and at another time *variable.* Now if this axiom be admitted, and likewise the *first*, viz. that everything which *has* happened has occurred in conformity with a fixed law, it follows that the *third* and last proposition must be rejected, viz. that *that* which neither *has occurred*, nor will *occur*, yet might happen, for, if it did, it could only be fortuitously, but by the first proposition *past* events are admitted *not* to be fortuitous, therefore by the second no *event* can be fortuitous. Q.E.D." Here we have the doctrine of absolute necessity maintained by the Megaric school, and especially by its most illustrious representative, Diodorus Cronus. The Stoics Zeno and Cleanthes, it seems, admitted the *second* and *third* propositions, and therefore rejected the *first;* for, by admitting the third, they virtually allowed the *fortuitousness* of future events, and therefore, by the second, they were compelled to deny the *necessity* of the past, and thus abandoned the idea of fate altogether. Chrysippus, however, although a Stoic, attempted to cut the logical knot by which this argument was connected, for he refused to admit the validity of the *second* proposition, and thus was left to the alternative of allowing that the past was *necessary*, but that the future might be to a certain degree *fortuitous*. We have already explained, in the preceding chapter, by what process of reasoning Chrysippus arrived at this result, viz. by the adoption of the principle of confatalism, or auxiliary causes. This notion, which in substance was held by the Epicureans as well as by the Stoics, was perhaps more intelligibly, although quaintly, illustrated by the former. Cicero tells us that Epicurus, when he found, if his *atoms* were allowed to descend by their own weight, our actions could not be in our power, because their motions would be certain and necessary, invented an expedient which had escaped Democritus, to avoid necessity. He says, that when the atoms descend by their own weight, or gravity, they move a little obliquely: " Ait atomum, cum pondere et gravitate directo deorsum feratur, declinare paululum [1]." Now, although in the context to the above passage it appears that Cotta considered this argument so despicable, that he affirms Epicurus could

[1] *De Nat. Deor.* I. 25.
" Illud in his quoque te rebus cognoscere avemus,
corpora cum deorsum rectum per inane feruntur,
ponderibus propriis incerto tempore ferme
incertisque loci spatiis decellere paulum,
tantum quod momen mutatum dicere possis.
Quod nisi declinare solerent, omnia deorsum,
Imbris uti guttæ, caderent per inane profundum,
nec foret offensus natus nec plaga creata
principiis: ita nil umquam natura creasset."
Lucretius, II. 216—224.

only have advanced it for the sake of affording his adversary the gratification of an easy victory, yet it seems to us susceptible of explanation and application to the subject under discussion, although perhaps more appreciable to a mathematician than to a logician. The oblique direction of the atoms was a crude notion of a resultant force which might have an infinite number of pairs of components, which again might be compounded in an infinite number of ways, and therefore the successive changes in nature would appear fortuitous, although subject to the operation of immutable laws of force, *whereas* vertical resultants would, as it were, be susceptible of no reciprocal action, and therefore must continue to act in the direction of the force primarily impressed on them[1]. The attempt of Chrysippus, as we have seen, to reconcile the idea of a fixed law in the order of things, with that of the spontaneity of the human agent, was founded on somewhat similar reasoning, viz. the cooperation and coefficiency of causes. That this expedient did not fulfil the end desired, is logically and clearly demonstrated by Carneades, whose arguments Cicero has recorded in his treatise *De Fato*, one of the most elegant and luminous fragments of the great author's works. After relating the Stoical and Megaric logomachies on the subject of free will and necessity, "Carneades," he continues, "rejected

[1] "Denique si semper motus conectitur omnis
et vetere exoritur *semper* novus ordine certo,
nec declinando faciunt primordia motus
principium quoddam quod fati foedera rumpat,
ex infinito ne causam causa sequatur,
libera per terras unde hæc animantibus exstat,
unde est hæc, inquam, fatis avolsa potestas
per quam progredimur quo ducit quemque voluntas,
declinamus item motus nec tempore certo
nec regione loci certa, sed ubi ipsa tulit mens?
nam dubio procul his rebus sua cuique voluntas
principium dat et hinc motus per membra rigantur."
Lucretius, II. 251—262.

these methods of reasoning, and considers their conclusions are adopted too hastily. He therefore pushed his argument in a plainer manner, and avoided these subtleties. 'If,' says he, 'everything happens by anterior causes, all these causes must be closely and compactly bound to each other by a natural connexion. Now if this is the case, necessity governs all things; we are no longer free agents; nothing is in our own power. But some things are in our own power; but if all things happen by fate, then all things happen by anterior causes: therefore all that happens does not happen by fate.'" Carneades thus shows that an eternal concatenation of causes is incompatible with the idea of a free agency; and that the Stoical doctrine on this point leaves the question unsolved.

We find the real difficulty underlying all these consequences about fate and necessity to have been the utter inability of the disputants to conceive anything as *possible in existence* which was *impossible in thought*. Thus the great crux in the question of free will was the inconceivability of an effect without any apparent cause. Whence proceeded that determination of the mind which we call the act of volition? In conformity with the materialism of the Stoics it must originate externally to the mind. But this was as illogical, or as little conformable to the idea of free will, as an independent effect was to the idea of causation. The only legitimate solution was to suppose the existence in man of an absolutely free, independent, and active principle, having no attribute in common with matter, and whose very essence was the power of originating motion. It was in support of this opinion that Carneades and the later Academicians were most decidedly opposed to the Stoics. As we have already explained how the Epicureans attempted to parry the consequences of their own mechanical hypotheses, the following reasoning[1] of Carneades will be easily under-

---

[1] *De Fato*, XI.

stood: "Acutius Carneades, qui docebat, posse Epicureos suam causam sine hac commentitia declinatione defendere. Nam cum doceret esse posse quendam animi motum voluntarium, id fuit defendi melius, quam introducere declinationem, cujus praesertim causam reperire non possunt. Quo defenso, facile Chrysippo possent resistere. Cum enim concessissent, motum nullum esse sine causa, non concederent, omnia, quae fierent, fieri causis antecedentibus: voluntatis enim nostrae non esse causas externas, et antecedentes. Communi igitur consuetudine sermonis abutimur, cum ita dicimus, velle aliquid quempiam aut nolle sine causa. Ita enim dicimus, *sine causa*, ut dicamus, sine externa et antecedenti causa, non sine aliqua.—Motus enim voluntarius cam naturam in se ipse continet, ut sit in nostra potestate, nobisque pareat: nec id sine causa ejus enim rei causa, ipsa natura est." Here we have a clear and explicit statement of the nature of a free agent, and subsequent exposition has contributed little to the illumination of the subject. Those who maintain that the act must follow the strongest motive, and that *that* motive must be primarily extrinsic, do but echo the opinions of Chrysippus, while, on the other hand, the conclusions of those who uphold the pure spontaneity of the voluntary act apart from appetite or deliberation, were already articulately announced by Carneades and the later Academicians. It was indeed the radical and substantial difference of their views on this point that constitutes the irreconcileable divergence of the two schools. To recognise a self-acting determining principle in the individual man, was but to see the reflection of an analogous power in the universe; and to him who was conscious of the presence of a spontaneous intelligent faculty in himself, it would not be illogical to conceive a Deity with similar attributes presiding over and originating the order of nature. We have seen that the theory of perception adopted by the Stoics was implicitly involved *in*, and naturally issued *from*, the passivity of the perceiving subject. Sir William Hamilton indeed makes Pantheism the corollary of that theory which admits the equipoise of the subject-object in the act of perception[1]. It seems, however, probable that at least in the case of the Stoics this order was reversed, and the notion of the comprehension of the object by the subject in perception was a necessary consequence from their Pantheistic principles. The fundamental idea indeed of Pantheism, viz. "that a cause cannot produce an effect unlike itself," seems naturally to suggest an intuitive theory of perception, where the representative image or modification of consciousness exactly measures its external cause.

§ ε. Carneades, we shall see, as in theology and logic, propounded a diametrically opposite view concerning the nature and limits of human knowledge to that of the Stoics; substituting, for the ultra-objectivism of the latter, an equally uncompromising idealism, which allowed in the subjective object of perception nothing but a vicarious representation or indication of the external cause. The opinions of Carneades, in opposition to the cataleptic phantasm of the Stoics, have been preserved to us by Sextus Empiricus; and as his account of them is brief, explicit, and comprehensive, we shall give a translation of those passages of his work, *Contra Mathematicos*, in which it is contained[2]: "But Carneades was opposed on the question of the criterion of knowledge to all preceding him. His *first* argument was of a more general nature, in which he showed that there is no absolute criterion of truth; neither reason, nor sensation, imagination, nor anything else. But all these things, in short, deceive us. *Secondly*, he differed from preceding philosophers, inasmuch as he demonstrated, that even if there were this criterion it

---

[1] Reid's *Works* (Hamilton). Note A. § 1. p. 749, I. "If the veracity," &c.
[2] *Contra Mathematicos*, VII. 159—161.

could not exist apart from the act of consciousness. Now an animal differs from inanimate objects in having sensuous susceptibility, through which it becomes a percipient of itself and external objects. But as long as sensation is unaroused, dormant, and unaffected, neither is it sensation, nor is it a percipient of anything. But being excited and provoked in any way by the incidence of material objects, then it shows us external things. The criterion, therefore, must be sought in the act of consciousness (ἐν ἄρα τῷ ἀπὸ τῆς ἐνεργείας πάθει). But the act must be indicative of the subject itself, and also of the subject-object (τοῦτο δὲ τὸ πάθος αὐτοῦ ἐνδεικτικὸν ὀφείλει τυγχάνειν καὶ τοῦ ἐμποιήσαντος αὐτὸ φαινομένου), which act then is inseparable from the image, object of thought, or subject-object (ὅπερ πάθος ἐστὶν οὐχ ἕτερον τῆς φαντασίας)." Into the above section[1] is condensed an entire theory of perception: a theory differing little from that of Reid, and Brown, and which Sir William Hamilton calls the theory of Cosmothetic Idealism, or Hypothetical Realism[2]. In it we have to remark *four* distinct assertions, by which this theory is mainly distinguished.

✓ 1. The activity of the mind in perception is emphatically announced, the awakening to consciousness being termed the τὸ ἀπὸ τῆς ἐνεργείας πάθος.

[1] *Adv. Math.* VII. 161. Some read ἐναργείας for ἐνεργείας. To do this would be to beg the whole question at issue.

[2] Reid's *Works* (Hamilton). Note A. § 1. p. 749, IV. "If the testimony of consciousness to our *knowledge* of an external world existing be rejected with the Idealist, but with the Realist the *existence* of that world be affirmed, we have a scheme which, as it, by many various hypothesis, endeavours, on the one hand, not to give up the reality of an unknown material universe, and on the other, to explain the ideal illusion of its cognition, may be called the doctrine of Cosmothetic Idealism, Hypothetical Realism, or Hypothetical Dualism." Sir W. Hamilton would not admit that Reid and Brown held the same theory. Our limits forbid our entering upon the discussion of this point, which is exhaustively treated in Sir W. Hamilton's celebrated *Essay on Perception*.

✓ 2. It is expressly denied that there can be any consciousness apart from the conscious act[1], ἡ δέ γε αἴσθησις ἀκίνητος μένουσα καὶ ἀπαθὴς καὶ ἄτρεπτος οὔτε αἴσθησίς ἐστιν οὔτε ἀντιληπτική τινος. Aristotle had already anticipated this obvious and philosophical conclusion, from which, as we know, Reid, and some later French writers, have differed.

✓ 3. Carneades recognises nothing in the mental image but a phenomenal representation of its cause, a mere effect in which we are conscious of nothing but the presence (ὑπόπτωσιν) of the external object. But the object of thought is not the external object, *but* that which stands for it in the mind (τοῦ ἐμποιήσαντος αὐτὸ φαινομένου).

✓ 4. Is enunciated the observation that the *act* of perception is identical with the *object* of thought, ὅπερ πάθος ἐστὶν οὐχ ἕτερον τῆς φαντασίας.

Here then we see already detected that identity of the act and object of perception which Sir William Hamilton reiterates was never noticed before M. Crousaz, the whole credit of which he attributes to Reid[2]. But to return to Sextus Empiricus[3]: "Whence we may say that a mental presentation (φαντασία) is a sort of consciousness in an animal, making the animal aware of its own existence, and the existence of that which aroused it. As Antiochus remarks, 'When we look at an object we are conscious somehow of vision, and feel the sense of vision to be in a different state to what it was before we looked at the object (προσβλέψαντές τινι, διατιθέμεθά πως τὴν ὄψιν, καὶ οὐχ οὕτως αὐτὴν δια-

---

[1] "Consciousness is not to be regarded as aught different from the mental modes or movements themselves. It is not to be viewed as an illuminated place, within which objects coming are presented to, and passing beyond are withdrawn from, observation; nor is it to be considered as an observer—the mental modes as phænomena observed."—Reid's *Works* (Hamilton). Note H. p. 932. Brown's *Lecture on Consciousness*. Hamilton's *Essay on Perception*.

[2] Hamilton's *Essay on Perception*.

[3] *Adv. Math.* VII. 162.

κειμένην ἴσχομεν ὡς πρὶν τοῦ βλέψαι διακειμένην εἴχομεν).'
In fact, however, we are conscious of two things in this modification.
1. The modification itself.
2. The thing seen, or that which constructs the modification; and similarly of the other senses. As light both shows itself, and everything around it, so the mental modification being the originator of consciousness in an animal, as an illumination displays itself, and also the subject-object which caused it. But since it does not always report its object according to truth, but often lies, and differs from the objects which caused it, like sorry messengers, it follows necessarily that, not every representation can afford a criterion, but only that which is true, *if there be a true one*. Again, no appearance is so true but that it might be false, *and* corresponding to every one apparently true *there may be* a false one indistinguishable from it. The criterion, therefore, will not *primâ facie* distinguish the true from the false[1]. But an appearance partaking of both the true and the false cannot be comprehensive (καταληπτική), and not being comprehensive, cannot be a criterion. No phantasm being capable of deciding, neither can reason be a criterion; for the reports of sense are the materials of reason. For that which is judged of must first be brought before the reason, but nothing can appear to the reason without the intervention of the senses[2]. Neither then is there a criterion in reason, nor in sensation."
It is impossible to understand the controversy about the cri-

[1] "παραλαβὼν ἀληθεῖ μὲν ὅμοιον ψεῦδος, καταληπτικῇ δὲ φαντασίᾳ καταληπτὸν ὅμοιον, καὶ ἀγαγὼν εἰς τὰς ἴσας οὐκ εἴασεν οὔτε τὸ ἀληθὲς εἶναι οὔτε τὸ ψεῦδος, ἢ οὐ μᾶλλον τὸ ἕτερον τοῦ ἑτέρου, ἢ μᾶλλον ἀπὸ τοῦ πιθανοῦ."—*Numenius* apud *Eusebium*, 14. 8.

[2] " Quid majore fide porro quam sensus haberi
debet? an ab sensu falso ratio orta valebit
dicere eos contra, quæ tota ab sensibus orta est?
qui nisi sunt veri, ratio quoque falsa fit omnis."
                                        Lucretius, IV. 482—485.

terion of truth, without having a distinct appreciation of the nature of the problem to be solved, although it is not evident, from the discussions recorded, that the exact nature of the question was ever perceived by either party of the disputants. What then was this criterion of truth, or rather, what was truth? Truth seems to have meant the reality of the existence of the object of thought in perception: the agreement of the φαινόμενον with the ὑποκείμενον, of the *objectum quo* with the *objectum quod*. Now it is evident in every representative theory of perception, *where* the object of thought only affords a mediate cognition of the object in existence, that the degree of this reality or truth can only be hypothetical. For, as the Sceptics continually urged, unless one could see the *external object*, independent of its *representation* in the *mind*, how is it possible to know that they are conformable to one another? How can you assert that the picture of Socrates is like him, unless you have seen Socrates himself? But who has ever transcended the sphere of consciousness, who has ever seen things but as ideas in the mind? and if this comparison of the idea and the thing is impossible, where is the criterion of truth? By such reasoning Carneades denied the possibility of a criterion; but the fact was, the Stoics never asserted that in this sense there was any. For, as we have seen, their theory of perception, although partly representative, was analogous to that which we should *now* term *immediate cognition*, where the knowledge is of the thing itself, the *objectum quod*, and therefore involves the *fact* of its existence[1]. The very definition of the cataleptic phantasm implied its comprehension, or perfect representation of the object; and its fidelity was founded upon the logical conception of causation. The real superiority of the opinions of Carneades over those of the Stoics

---

[1] Reid's *Works*, Hamilton. Note B. § 1. 1. p. 805.

with respect to the question of knowledge was, the consistent maintenance by the former of an active principle in the mind, the real subject of cognition. The existence of such a principle of intelligence is implied in the passages quoted above from Sextus Empiricus, as in the expression τὸ ἀπὸ τῆς ἐνεργείας πάθος, indicating the fact that in perception, *although* the mind may be passive in respect to the external causes of its modifications, *yet* that cognition or knowledge is an act implying the presence of an independent agent. This doctrine is, however, more explicitly announced, though apparently not very clearly understood, by Cicero, who, while controverting the doctrine of probabilities propounded by Carneades and the later Academicians, makes the following remark: "Simili in errore versantur, cum convicti, ac vi veritatis coacti, perspicua a perceptis volunt distinguere, et conantur ostendere, esse aliquid perspicui, verum illud quidem impressum in animo atque mente, neque tamen id percipi ac comprehendi posse[1]." The distinction taken here between *perspicua* and *percepta* is radical and substantial. *Perspicua* distinguishes the act of cognition from *percepta*, mere passive impressions on the mind, but not necessarily implying knowledge. A *percept* then, according to Carneades, was nothing but a modification of the mind determined by some unknown external cause, and a *perspect* was the active recognition of this modification by the dianoetic faculty, a power in the mind which materialists have never admitted. The limits of human knowledge appear to have been thus determined by Carneades. The mind was

[1] Lucullus, 11. To understand this point fully we must refer the reader to the discussion on the subject in the *Theætetus*, p. 185 u. Σκόπει γάρ, ἀπόκρισις ποτέρα ὀρθοτέρα, ᾧ ὁρῶμεν, τοῦτο εἶναι ὀφθαλμοὺς, ἢ δι' οὗ ὁρῶμεν, καί, ᾧ ἀκούομεν, ὦτα, ἢ δι' οὗ ἀκούομεν. ΘΕΑΙ. Δι' ὧν ἕκαστα αἰσθανόμεθα, ἔμοιγε δοκεῖ, ὦ Σώκρατες, μᾶλλον ἢ οἷς. ΣΟ. Δεινὸν γάρ που, ὦ παῖ, εἰ πολλαί τινες ἐν ἡμῖν, ὥσπερ ἐν δουρείοις ἵπποις, αἰσθήσεις ἐγκάθηνται, ἀλλὰ μὴ εἰς μίαν τινὰ ἰδέαν, εἴτε ψυχὴν, εἴτε ὃ δεῖ καλεῖν, πάντα ταῦτα ξυντείνει· ᾗ διὰ τούτων οἷον ὀργάνων αἰσθανόμεθα ὅσα αἰσθητά, κ.τ.λ.

competent to weigh, compare and judge its own ideas, and detect their agreement or disagreement. But the external causes of those ideas he declared to be incomprehensible (ἀκατάληπτον), or imperceptible, 'still he left to man more than he took from him;' for the Stoics, in giving man the faculty of the immediate cognition of external objects, at the same time deprived him of any agency in the process. But Carneades, although proclaiming that our ideas were only the indications, and not the resemblances of things, yet allowed the subject the power of the free and deliberate comparison of them. The Stoics found in man a feeling of conviction, certainty or assent, which the mind accorded to the results of its own operations; but they made this belief or assent only an involuntary and necessary acquiescence in a scarcely more than mechanical law. Whereas Carneades, although he maintained the uncertainty and inadequateness of our knowledge of the existence or relations of things beyond the sphere of consciousness, still allowed man the power of intelligently estimating the value of evidence and the degree of probability.

§ ζ. This doctrine of probability which, as distinguished from certainty, produces *belief* as the latter *knowledge*, is by most writers considered as the eminent and essential characteristic of the teaching of Carneades. But Cicero in commencing the defence of his school against Lucullus asserts that sages had always admitted a degree of knowledge short of certainty. "Nemo, unquam, superiorum non modo expresserat, sed ne dixerat quidem, posse hominem nihil opinari: nec solum posse, sed ita necesse esse sapienti[1]." Still as the only and sufficient ground of action, the validity of probable evidence separates the school of Carneades most completely, in theory at least, from the contemporary dogmatic, as well as sceptical sects of philosophers. In a con-

[1] Lucullus, 24.

tinuation of the passages already quoted from Sextus Empiricus we are enabled to gather the opinions of Carneades on the subject of probability[1]. "Carneades asserting these things against the other philosophers, demonstrated the impossibility of any criterion of truth, but when pressed for some criterion in the conduct of life, or the pursuit of happiness, was compelled to admit the virtual existence of such a rule, taking the simply probable perception, and that perception which, besides being probable, is disturbed by no doubt, but is evident and clear (καὶ τὴν πιθανὴν ἅμα καὶ ἀπερίσπαστον καὶ διεξωδευμένην). What then is the difference between such perceptions we will briefly consider. A mental image or representation (ἡ φαντασία) may be considered in relation either to the *object* it represents, or to the *subject* to whom it represents it, the *object* (τὸ φανταστόν) being something external to the mind, the *subject* (ὁ φαντασιούμενος) being man[2]. According to the relation of the image with its object, the perception is true or false. It is true whenever it is conformable to its object, and false when not. In relation to the subject the image *appears* to be either true or false. That perception which *appears* true is called by the Academicians *emphasis* (ἔμφασις), probability, or a probable perception. And that which does not *appear* true is called ἀπέμφασις, improbability, or the improbable perception. For neither that which is evidently false, nor that which, although true, does not appear so, is adapted to convince us. Now, that which *appears true*, and *appears sufficiently clearly*, is a criterion according to the followers of Carneades. Since no phantasm comes singly, but one follows another in a sort of chain, there will be a second criterion, the *probable* and *unopposed* phantasm[3]. For when one distinguishes a man

---

[1] *Adv. Math.* VII. 166, 167, 168, 169, 173, 176.

[2] Cf. *Philebus*, 254. 255. "δοξα, δοξαζον, δοξαζομενον."

[3] "Probabilis visio et quæ non impediatur."—Lucullus, 11. "Probabile neque ulla re impeditum."—*l. l.* 31.

one necessarily perceives those things which belong to a man, as complexion, height, figure, &c.[1], and those which environ him, as the air, sky, earth, &c. Whenever then none of these accessories induce us to doubt, but all are equally credible, we are naturally inclined to believe the evidence of our senses. Again, still more worthy of credit and probable in a higher degree is that complex perception, which, besides having all its parts consistent with each other, has each of those parts probable and trustworthy in itself. Such a perception we shall next describe. For a *second* degree of probability we only require that each element of a complex conception shall be consistent with the whole, and that they all should appear true and not improbable. But in a probable conception of the *third* degree we examine each part separately somehow, as is done in the election of public functionaries, when the claims of each candidate are examined for the purpose of determining who is worthy to be a magistrate or ruler." These *three* degrees of probability are elsewhere illustrated by Sextus Empiricus thus[2]. They, the New Academicians, say that *some* perceptions are barely probable ($\pi\iota\theta\alpha\nu\grave{\alpha}\varsigma$), that *others* are probable, and after consideration deserving of belief ($\pi\iota\theta\alpha\nu\grave{\alpha}\varsigma$ καὶ διεξωδευμένας), and that a *third* sort are almost convincing ($\pi\iota\theta\alpha\nu\grave{\alpha}\varsigma$ καὶ περιωδευμένας καὶ ἀπερισπάστους). As for example, to one suddenly entering a darkened chamber the appearance of a rope lying on the floor would suggest the idea of a snake[3]; this would be a *probable* perception. *Secondly*, after a consideration of the circumstances attending the phenomenon, such as this thing does not move, is of such a colour, &c., the rope stands revealed as far as a probable and plausible impression

[1] Lecture IV. page 73, note 1.
[2] *Hyp.* I. 33. 227.
[3] Καὶ ὅταν τοίνυν τῷ μὲν παρῇ αἴσθησις τῶν σημείων, τῷ δὲ μὴ, τὸ δὲ τῆς ἀπούσης αἰσθήσεως τῇ παρούσῃ προσαρμόσῃ, πάντῃ ταύτῃ ψεύδεται ἡ διάνοια."— *Theætetus*, 194, a.

goes (φαίνεται σχοινίον κατὰ τὴν φαντασίαν τὴν πιθανὴν καὶ περιωδευμένην). As an instance of the *third* degree of probability, Hercules, it is said, brought back from Hades the dead Alcestis, and showed her to Admetus, and he recognised the image of Alcestis after accurate consideration, although, since he knew that she had died, his mind was not disposed to consent, but more inclined to be incredulous. This notion of *probabilities* was really an attempt on the part of Carneades to compromise between the absolute scepticism of the Pyrrhonists, and the stolid dogmatism of the Stoics. Where there is no criterion or canon of truth, said the *former*, all our perceptions being only appearances and not facts are equally true or equally false. Our perceptions, the *latter* maintained, being cognitions of facts immediate and direct, carry with them their own evidence, and require no other criterion. Our perceptions, said Carneades, are appearances, not facts, but the evidence of facts; and there is a faculty in the mind by which we are enabled to estimate the force of this evidence, and to yield to conviction when reason has been satisfied with the proofs. But, replies the Stoic, if you deny me the power of detecting the true from the false in my judgment of facts, by what standard or criterion can you pronounce that sufficient evidence has been obtained to make a perception probable or improbable? For why admit the ability of estimating the probable when you deny that of judging of the truth? "Quamobrem, sive tu probabilem visionem, sive probabilem et quæ non impediatur, ut Carneades volebat, sive aliud quid proferes, quod sequare: ad visum illud, de quo agimus, tibi erit revertendum (scilicet καταληπτικὴ φαντασία[1])." The question was really limited to that second solution in the Theætetus, that time-honoured enquiry, What is knowledge? Knowledge is right judgment (ὀρθὸς λόγος), and so the dilemma which this question was

[1] Lucullus, 11.

propounded to intensify, was not evaded by the probabilities of Carneades. To weigh evidence is the function of reason, but according to what idea shall that evidence be declared to be sufficient or insufficient, conclusive or inconclusive? Hence it has been maintained by some writers that Carneades taught esoterically the Platonic doctrines[1]. We should think, however, that it was not so much the Platonic idea that was preserved by Carneades, but merely that belief in, or reliance on, those original instincts of the intellect which constitutes the foundation of all reasoning. It seems indeed to require no *à priori* idea to enable the mind to determine that the corroborating evidence of a dozen independent witnesses approaches nearer to demonstration than the unsupported testimony of one. And that, although the veracity of each taken singly might be doubted, the chance that they would all unite in a falsehood would be less than the probability that they were reporting a truth. Our cognition of an external object is really the complex idea of *it*, of which each of its qualities, attributes, or accidents, is a component, and each is an independent witness, by which we may identify the object[2]. Nature has provided us with such testimony by allowing us to discern a separate quality in everything through each sense, making as it were a sort of natural and voluntary analysis of things. But, says the Sceptic, senses deceive; they do not tell you of anything in the object—you only perceive changes in your own consciousness—perhaps so —but at least these changes must have an external cause. When, then, many sensations are united in *one* object, their presence is cumulative evidence of the presence of the object which is their cause, and the greater the number of witnesses, the more convincing will be their corroborating testimony. Hence we can see the utility of increasing the number of the

[1] Eusebius *Præp. Ev.* xiv. 38.
[2] Aristotle, *de Anima*, lib. iii. 1.

components of our complex perception of an object, by adding, to the *natural analysis* of the senses, the *artificial analysis* of experiment, by which we interrogate nature, and by the process of induction arrive *at least*, if not at a *knowledge* of the secrets of her combinations, at a *high* degree of *probability*. The reader will find the subject of probabilities treated from the common sense point of view, as the only possible, and at the same time perfectly adequate rule of action, by Cicero in Lucullus. "Etenim is quoque, qui a vobis sapiens inducitur, multa sequitur probabilia, non comprehensa neque percepta, neque assensa, sed similia veri, quæ nisi probet, omnis vita tollatur. Quid enim? conscendens navem sapiens num comprehensum animo habet atque perceptum, se ex sententia navigaturum, &c.[1]"

§ η. We have, we trust, indicated with sufficient detail the opinions of Carneades on those *four* points with respect to which the views of the New Academy seem most decidedly hostile to those of the Stoics. We have not indeed alluded to their views on the subject of morality, principally because it would be difficult to pronounce on this topic, which of the later Academicians we ought to consider as representing the sentiments of this school. Cicero, who on every point of speculative philosophy seems to have adhered to the method, and approved perhaps of the teachings of Carneades, on questions of morality was diametrically opposed to the apparent views of Carneades and his followers: "Perturbatricem autem harum omnium rerum Academiam, hanc ab Arcesila et Carneade recentem, exoremus, ut sileat. Nam si invaserit in hæc, quæ satis scite nobis instructa et composita videntur, nimias edet ruinas. Quam quidem ego placare cupio, submovere non audeo[2]." It seems, however, most probable that the opinions expressed

---

[1] Lucullus, 31. [2] Cicero, *de Legibus*, I. 13.

by Carneades on the instability of moral distinctions, in direct opposition to the absolute nature of the obligations of virtue maintained by the more positive schools of philosophy, were only a manifestation of that general hostility which he constantly exhibited towards the Stoics. And there is no reason to suppose, that while attacking the immutability of the fundamental principles of morality putatively fixed by the order of nature, he did not secretly adhere to the traditions of the Older Academy, wherein Plato had propounded the existence of a good beyond and above nature, the manifestation of eternal laws and causes[1]. It would indeed have been utterly at variance with the spirit of the rest of his teaching for Carneades to have admitted the possibility of generalising certain and ultimate principles of good and evil, from observations of the conformity or nonconformity of actions to the intentions of nature. Therefore, for those who would allow none but empirical sources of knowledge, he consistently maintained the subjective character of all human conceptions of right

[1] "Truth in the power, or faculty, is nothing else but a conformity of its conceptions or Ideas unto the natures and relations of things, which in God we may call an actual, steady, immoveable, eternal Omniformity, as Plotinus calls the Divine Intellect, ἐν πάντα, which you have largely described by him. And this the Platonists truly call the Intellectual World, for here are the natures of all things pure and unmixed, purged from all those dregs, refined from all that dross and alloy which cleave unto them in their particular instances. All inferior and sublunary things, not excluding Man himself, have their excrescences, and defects. Exorbitances or privations are moulded up in their very frames and constitutions. There is somewhat extraneous, heterogeneous, and preternatural in all things here below, as they exist among us; but in that other world like the most purely fined gold, they shine in their native and proper glory. Here is the first goodness, the benign Parent of the whole Creation, with his numerous offspring, the infinite throng of Created Beings. Here is the fountain of Eternal Law, with all its streams and rivulets. Here is the Sun of uncreated glory surrounded with all his rays and beams. Here are the eternal indispensable Laws of Right and Justice, the immediate and indemonstrable principles of truth and goodness."
—Dr Rust, *A Discourse on Truth*, Sect. XVIII.

and wrong, and decided that prudence and utility were the only criteria of good and evil. With regard to the successors of Carneades, Philo seems to have denied the validity of the cataleptic phantasm as a criterion of truth, but yet to have asserted that knowledge could attain to the nature of things : "οἱ δὲ περὶ Φίλωνά φασιν, ὅσον μὲν ἐπὶ τῷ Στωϊκῷ κριτηρίῳ, τουτέστι τῇ καταληπτικῇ φαντασίᾳ, ἀκατάληπτα εἶναι τὰ πράγματα, ὅσον δὲ ἐπὶ τῇ φύσει τῶν πραγμάτων αὐτῶν κατάληπτα¹." This statement favours the impression that Philo more emphatically supported the traditions of the Old Academy. We can only have cognition of things *per se* either by means of the cataleptic phantasm or through *à priori* ideas. The former source was explicitly rejected by Philo, he therefore must have reserved the latter. Antiochus, after having been a stanch upholder of the Academic method, seems to have finally compromised with the Stoics, and thus brought the long polemic between them and the Academy to a close : "ὁ Ἀντίοχος τὴν Στοὰν μετήγαγεν εἰς τὴν Ἀκαδημίαν, ὡς καὶ εἰρῆσθαι ἐπ' αὐτῷ ὅτι ἐν Ἀκαδημίᾳ φιλοσοφεῖ τὰ Στωϊκά· ἐπεδείκνυε γὰρ ὅτι παρὰ Πλάτωνι κεῖται τὰ τῶν Στωϊκῶν δόγματα²." The victory then would appear to have ultimately rested with the dogmatists. The *judicium incogniti et cogniti*—the point about which the whole controversy had eddied—seems at last to have confounded and interchanged with the Platonic idea, and thus a ground of certainty was admitted as a principle of human knowledge.

Still from the writings of Cicero we might infer that this positivism did not extend beyond the region of ethical

---

¹ *Hyp.* I. 235, chap. 33.
² *Hyp.* I. 33. 235. "Licetne per ipsum Antiochum? Qui appellabatur Academicus: erat quidem, si perpauca mutavisset, germanissimus Stoicus."—Lucullus, 43.

enquiries; and in physical and metaphysical speculations a tendency to eclecticism is apparent, which is generally significant of a relapse into utter scepticism: "Horum aliquid vestro sapienti certum videtur: nostro, ne quid maxime quidem probabile sit, occurrit. Ita sunt in plerisque contrariarum rationum paria momenta[1]."

[1] Lucullus, 40.

LECTURE VI.

IDEALISM AND SCEPTICISM—ANCIENT AND RECENT.

"Die menschliche Vernunft ist so baulustig, dass sie mehrmalen schon den Thurm aufgeführt, hernach aber wieder abgetragen hat, um zu sehen, wie das Fundament desselben wohl beschaffen seyn möchte."

§ *a.* WE have now, we trust, dwelt sufficiently long on the details of our subject to enable you to form some notion of the spirit and method of ancient Scepticism, both as exhibited in its extreme form by Pyrrho and his followers, as well as in its partial manifestation under the representatives of the New Academy. We shall proceed to take a general view of the doctrines of these two schools, for the purpose of comparing their opinions and influence, in conformity with the object of our lectures. The positions of Scepticism were reduced to *five*, by Agrippa, a later representative of Pyrrhonism, which have been preserved to us by Sextus Empiricus, as the πέντε τρόποι[1]. In these are comprised all the arguments the most advanced Sceptics have urged against the probative force of all evidence, hence, against the possibility

[1] *Hyp.* I. 15. 164.

of man's attaining by mediate or indirect means any certain knowledge whatever. The *first* argument is derived from the discrepancy of opinion (ὁ ἀπὸ τῆς διαφωνίας) observable both amongst philosophers and the vulgar, in consequence of which inconsistency the Sceptic has no alternative but to suspend his judgment on all points. *Secondly*, every process of demonstration must be continued to infinity (ὁ ἀπὸ τῆς εἰς ἄπειρον ἐκπτώσεως), for all evidence requires other evidence to attest its validity; therefore proof would demand proof without end. The *third* is founded on the relativity of all our knowledge (ὁ ἀπὸ τοῦ πρός τι). For we can only affirm that anything is such as it appears, either to ourselves or with respect to surrounding objects, but of its absolute and independent nature we can assert nothing. The *fourth* position is directed against the assumption of general indemonstrable principles (ὁ ἐξ ὑποθέσεως), from which all reasoning must commence, or be reduced to an infinite regression. *Fifth* is the diallel (ὁ διάλληλος τρόπος)—*petitio principii*—the fallacy of circle[1], or the method of showing that a proof which is employed to establish the truth of a proposition, can itself only be proved by the proposition in question: as for example, "if anyone should infer the authenticity of a certain history, from its recording *such* and *such facts*, the *reality* of which rests on the evidence of that history." The Sceptics had not much difficulty in proving that every imaginable case not an object of immediate cognition could be brought under one or other of these objections, therefore all demonstration was fallacious, all truth impossible of attainment; not because anything could be demonstrated to be false, but because there was no faculty in the human intellect which could decide on the validity of its own operations. Such was the length and breadth of absolute scepticism, as propounded by the Pyrrho-

---

[1] Whately's *Logic. Of Fallacies*, Book III. 13.

nists. Let us now offer a few remarks on their doctrines separately, before viewing them in connection with those of the other school of thinkers which stands at the head of our subject.

§ β. *First*, we will examine some erroneous opinions prevalent even among the more enlightened respecting the real nature and tendency of Ancient Scepticism. It is not uncommon to hear urged as a triumphant refutation of Pyrrhonism, that, as a system of thought, it is self-annihilating and logically impossible[1]. Yet that this is not so, will we think be obvious, directly we understand the limits which the most absolute Sceptics have never transcended. The line indeed at which all scepticism, ancient or modern, must cease, is exactly *that* at which every school of later psychological and metaphysical speculatists have commenced. "Descartes recherche quel est le point de départ fixe et certain sur lequel peut s'appuyer la philosophie. Il se trouve que la pensée peut tout mettre en question, tout, excepté elle-même. En effet, quand on douterait de toutes choses, on pourrait au moins douter qu'on doute—or, douter c'est penser: d'où il suit qu'on ne peut douter qu'on pense, et que la pensée ne peut se renier elle-même, car elle ne le ferait qu'avec elle. Là est un cercle dont il est impossible à tout scepticisme de sortir; là est donc le point de départ ferme et certain cherché par Descartes; et comme la pensée nous est donnée dans la conscience, voilà la conscience prise comme le point de départ et le théâtre de toute recherche philosophique[2]."

"The facts of consciousness as mere phenomena, *facts* of which we have immediate and direct cognition, and to admit which

---

[1] "No conclusion can be drawn from it, viz., the inconceivability of the absolute, in favour of universal scepticism; first, because universal scepticism equally destroys itself, &c."—Mansel's *Bampton Lectures*, Lecture II. p. 59.

[2] Cousin, *Œuvres*, Vol. I. *Cours de l'histoire de la philosophie*. Onzième Leçon.

is merely to affirm the existence of consciousness itself, have never, and could never have been doubted, for doubt is itself a manifestation of consciousness[1]." To doubt whether we doubt, would be as contradictory as to be conscious of being unconscious. Scepticism therefore has always allowed the subjective reality of our mental presentations, and so far does not differ from the more positive schools of metaphysicians. To attempt then to force the Pyrrhonist to self-destruction in maintaining his own method is not feasible, since the *basis* of his system *is*, precisely *that consciousness* on the evidence of *which all truth must rest*. If Scepticism is suicidal, every other system is likewise. Similarly, we find in Eusebius an attempted answer to scepticism quoted from a work of Aristocles founded upon the supposed inconsistency of the Pyrrhonian method : "'Επεὶ τοίνυν (sc. οἱ σκεπτικοὶ) ἐπίσης ἀδιάφορα πάντα φασὶν εἶναι, καὶ διὰ τοῦτο κελεύουσι μηδενὶ προστίθεσθαι, μηδὲ δοξάζειν, εἰκότως ἄν, οἶμαι, πύθοιτό τις αὐτῶν· 'Αρά γε διαμαρτάνουσιν οἱ διαφέρειν αὐτὰ νομίζοντες, ἢ οὔ; Πάντως γάρ, εἰ μὲν ἁμαρτάνουσιν, οὐκ ὀρθῶς ὑπολαμβάνοιεν ἄν. Ὥστε ἀνάγκη λέγειν αὐτοῖς εἶναί τινας τοὺς τὰ ψευδῆ περὶ τῶν ὄντων δοξάζοντας· αὐτοὶ τοίνυν εἶεν ἂν οἱ τἀληθῆ λέγοντες· οὕτω δὲ εἴη ἂν ἀληθές τι καὶ ψεῦδος. Εἰ δ' οὐχ ἁμαρτάνομεν οἱ πολλοί, τὰ ὄντα διαφέρειν οἰόμενοι, τί παθόντες ἐπιπλήττουσιν ἡμῖν; αὐτοὶ γὰρ ἁμαρτάνοιεν ἄν, ἀξιοῦντες μὴ διαφέρειν αὐτά[2]." But this manner of confuting the followers of Pyrrho seems as little to meet the real point at issue as that of the Cynic philosopher[3], who, when he heard the possibility of motion denied, got up and walked as a proof of its reality; whereas the apparent or phenomenal existence of motion had never been called in question. So when the Pyrrhonist maintained the indistinguishability (ἀδιάφορα) of all things,

---

[1] Hamilton's *Reid*, Note A. § 1. p. 744.
[2] Eusebius, *Præp. Ev.* XIV. 18. B.
[3] *Hyp.* III. 8. 66.

it was only by the contradiction of appearances that his assertion was corroborated. It was not then the existence of *distinctions* in *appearances* that the Sceptic denied, on the contrary, it was these *distinctions* which, although antithetical, were equipollent, and therefore prevented him from arriving at a decision. The words, τὰ ψευδῆ περὶ τῶν ὄντων, seem to obscure the real question; followed as they are by δοξάζοντας, they imply a contradiction. There can be no opinion about realities, for realities are *objects* of *knowledge*, not of *opinion*. Opinion implies subjectivity, and by *an ultimate law of consciousness* contradiction in appearance forces upon us the conviction of our ignorance of the fact. But the avowed impossibility of comprehending the objective fact, imports no inability to distinguish appearances as mere phenomena of consciousness. So with the subsequent reasoning of Aristocles, it is assumed, that the assertion of everything being unknown involves the notion of the existence of a faculty by which the known and the unknown can be distinguished, viz. the *judicium incogniti et cogniti*, or intellectual conscience. Now it is precisely through the absence of such a faculty that scepticism justifies itself; and to say that *nothing* certain is *known*, simply means that there is no criterion by which we can judge, when we *think* we *know*, whether *we know or not*.

This is the very essence of scepticism, when it insists upon our inability to attain certain knowledge of anything. Such ignorance does not refer to the *object* of knowledge, but to the *subject* knowing. In the same sense Professor Mansel says: "Contradiction, whatever may be its ultimate import, is in itself not a quality of things, but a mode in which they are viewed by the mind." So scepticism does not touch the *incognitum et cognitum*, but the *judicium incogniti et cogniti*. There is no assumption of knowledge in its absolute denial, because knowledge refers to its object or material; the denial to the knowledge itself, or the faculty of knowing. The employment of sceptical weapons, then, is not logically impossible; but can they be employed against all the operations of reason, with equal chance of success? Now, according to the admissions of the Sceptics themselves, our *ideas*, as mere modes of consciousness, are intuitive facts; so must therefore be the *conclusions* which may be deduced from the comparison and judgment of those facts. Those *ideas* Locke calls the ideas of reflection, the archetypes of which are in the mind itself. Hence mathematical truths were not attacked by the Pyrrhonists, except in so far as any reasoning on the reality of things was attempted to be deduced from them. All abstractions indeed, inasmuch as they are abstractions, are necessarily phenomenal, subjective, and apparent. If then these form the only materials of our knowledge according to the idealist theory, Scepticism, after all, does but narrow the field of certain knowledge within the limits assigned to it by a large portion of modern thinkers. "Knowledge (says Locke) then seems to me to be nothing but the perception of the connexion and agreement, or disagreement and repugnancy, of any of our ideas. In this alone it consists. Where this perception is, there is knowledge; and where it is not, there, though we may fancy, guess, or believe, yet we always come short of knowledge[1]."

The position of Scepticism is also often represented as untenable because it is supposed to invalidate the illative processes of the understanding, and therefore destroy itself, or render the attempt nugatory, because, to disprove anything, we must make use of proofs and inferences. Thus Sextus Empiricus reports the arguments of the Dogmatists on this point:—" οἱ δὲ Δογματικοὶ τοὐναντίον κατασκευάζοντές φασιν, ὅτι ἤτοι ἀποδεικτικοί εἰσιν οἱ κατὰ τῆς ἀποδείξεως ἠρωτημένοι λόγοι ἢ οὐκ ἀποδεικτικοί. καὶ εἰ μὲν οὐκ ἀποδεικτικοί, οὐ δύναν-

[1] Locke, *Human Understanding*, Book IV. chap. I. 1.

ται δεικνύναι ὅτι οὐκ ἔστιν ἡ ἀπόδειξις· εἰ δὲ ἀποδεικτικοί εἰσιν, αὐτοὶ οὗτοι τὴν ὑπόστασιν τῆς ἀποδείξεως ἐκ περιτροπῆς εἰσάγουσιν[1]."

But it must be remarked that the real inferential force of an argument was strangely overlooked by the Stoical logicians, and therefore by the Sceptics, who invariably sought their opponents on their own ground. The truth of the hypothetical proposition, which was the organ of demonstration among the logicians of that time, was considered to be dependent on the truth or falsity of the propositions which formed the separate members, whereas, of course, the real probative power lies in the consequence[2]. This question, then, was obscured and confused by the antagonistic opinions of the Megaric and Stoical philosophers to such a degree, that the Sceptics had only too much occasion to throw doubt upon the whole process of demonstration. But it must be understood that it was only the artificial formulæ, and not the natural operations of the ratiocinative faculty, which they seemed to impugn. Perception of the agreement or disagreement of our ideas by the intervention of other ideas or media, being demonstrative[3], was not and could not be denied by the most extreme Sceptics; and when they oppose the conclusions of reason, as forming a sufficient ground for the rejection of both or the suspension of judgment, they do but obey that *first* principle of the reason by which we *cannot* conceive it possible for the *same thing to be* and *not to be*.

In the example Sextus Empiricus gives[4] of the apparent conflict of inferences, when to the conclusion—that there must be a Providence from the order observable in nature—it is opposed that the wicked are often prosperous, and the virtuous

---

[1] *Hyp.* II. 13. 185.
[2] *Elements of Logic*, Whately, Book II. chap. IV. § 3.
[3] Cf. Locke, *Human Understanding*, Book IV. chap. IV. 7.
[4] *Hyp.* I. 13. 32.

in adversity, *hence* that an inference might be drawn the exact opposite to the preceding, the real opposition is in the facts or premisses upon which the argument is based. It is therefore the inductive, and not the deductive process, which is here made a ground of doubt. And since induction, in as far as it means the observation and comparison of particulars without reference to the resulting generalization, is merely an operation of the judgment, scepticism cannot be said to attempt to subvert our belief in logical consequences. The *judicium incogniti et cogniti* in this case would be allowed as a subjective fact, proclaiming the inherent connexion of a conclusion with the premiss, in which the conclusion itself was originally involved. But how to establish the premiss, in the first place, is the problem to which all synthetical reasoning is ultimately reduced; and it is at this point that the five dilemmas of Agrippa, which constitute the principal *momenta* of scepticism, challenge the upholders of the ability of the human mind to comprehend and grasp the truth and reality of objective existence.

§ γ. "Aristotle (says Professor Maurice) to a great extent proclaimed the search for wisdom to be at an end. He left the impression on the minds of his disciples, that the whole scheme of the universe could be brought under the forms of the human understanding." Could any conclusion be more fatal than this to the cause of the advancement of human knowledge? Could any announcement be more provocative of the latent scepticism to which the Greek mind had always, by its peculiar constitution, been rendered more or less prone? It needed no special enquiry, either into the possible objects of knowledge, or the capabilities of the human instruments of cognition, at once to perceive that, if knowledge imported the apprehension of whatever was stable, real, essential, and causative, the Dogmatist had not even yet attained the first condition of all science, viz. *a con-*

sciousness *of its own nescience*. For how, urged the Sceptic, can he who imagines that his task is completed before it is even begun, expect to prosecute it with much advantage? If the province of the philosopher is but to verify a preconception, where is there any field for discovery? "ὅρα δὲ μὴ καὶ νῦν οἱ Δογματικοὶ ζητήσεως ἀπείργονται· οὐ γὰρ τοῖς ἀγνοεῖν τὰ πράγματα ὡς ἔχει πρὸς τὴν φύσιν ὁμολογοῦσι τὸ ζητεῖν ἔτι περὶ αὐτῶν ἀνακόλουθον, τοῖς δ' ἐπ' ἀκριβὲς οἰομένοις ταῦτα γιγνώσκειν. οἷς μὲν γὰρ ἐπὶ πέρας ἤδη πάρεστιν ἡ ζήτησις ὡς ὑπειλήφασιν, οἷς δὲ τὸ δι' ὃ πᾶσα συνίσταται ζήτησις ἀκμὴν ὑπάρχει, τὸ νομίζειν ὡς οὐχ εὑρήκασιν[1]." It would seem, therefore, that the systematization and articulate enunciation of the principles of Scepticism synchronised *with*, if they did not result *from*, the introduction of a scientific method into the processes of investigation. Thus, those who believed in, and those who discredited the ability of the intellect to penetrate the arcana of nature, were revealed to each other, and compelled to push their respective doctrines to lengths which equally menaced the existence of all philosophy. On the one hand the Stoics, the most dogmatic of the dogmatical schools after the age of Aristotle, pretended that, so far from admitting the incompetency of human reason to attain certainty of knowledge, all belief, or degree of assurance short of certitude, was unworthy of a wise man. On the other hand, the Pyrrhonist equally discarded belief, not as a degree of knowledge unworthy of a philosopher, but as unattainable by any one who could appreciate the force of evidence. So the characteristic distinction of Pyrrhonism or Scepticism *was*, the declaration of the inability of man to attain that *assurance* of *anything* which is entitled *belief*, owing to the *conflict* of *evidence* or *testimony* on which belief could *alone be grounded*. As a consequence of the opposition, and equal cogency of the reasons urged in *support* of and

[1] *Hyp.* II. 1. 11.

against any proposition, the mind, they said, *not* feeling itself determined in *one direction more than in another*, rested in a sort of equipoise or equilibrium, well known as the ἐποχή, or suspension of judgment. This ἐποχή is so identified *with*, and so essentially *the differential characteristic* of ancient scepticism, that it may be interesting to consider under what conditions, either with reference to the object of knowledge, or the subject knowing, such a mode of consciousness is possible. The term ἐπέχω is thus explicated by Sextus Empiricus[1]. "The word ἐπέχω is employed by us (viz. the Pyrrhonians) in the following signification: I am unable to declare what one should believe or not believe with respect to the objects of cognition (τῶν προκειμένων), meaning that things appear *equal* as to their credibility or incredibility. That they *are equal* we do not assert, only that they *appear* so subjectively and phenomenally when presented to us. The word ἐποχή imports retention or negation of judgment, εἴρηται ἀπὸ τοῦ ἐπέχεσθαι τὴν διάνοιαν, because we abstain from affirming or denying anything, on account of the equipollence (ἰσοσθένια) of evidence on which the proposition depends[2]." Thus the ἐποχή is a purely negative state of mind, equally removed from the attitude of belief or disbelief, yet somehow intermediate between the two. The avowed object of its adoption, as we have already seen, was to absent, as far as possible, all motive to action; but the Sceptics continually asserted that this state of suspension was not by any means voluntary, but was forced upon them by the consideration of the relations in which man stood to the materials of his consciousness. Thus the ἐποχή appears as the centre of the

---

[1] *Hyp.* I. 22. 196.

[2] "A proposition, as we have said before, is a portion of discourse in which a predicate is affirmed or denied of a subject."—Mill's *Logic*, Book I. chap. IV, 1. "We say of a fact or statement, that it is proved, when we believe its truth by reason of some other fact or statement from which it is said to *follow*."—Mill's *Logic*, Book II. chap. I. 1.

Sceptical philosophy, as determining its special peculiarities both with respect to speculative and practical science. For, on the one hand, it marked the speculative negativism of philosophical despair, and, on the other, it purported to be the instrument for the attainment of that apathy which must result from the removal of all motivity. The Sceptics themselves generally asserted that, in suspending their judgment on matters of doubtful evidence, they only followed the example of Socrates, whose maieutic method of discussion seemed to encourage the notion that he considered it the part of a philosopher to collect the opinions of others without forming any of his own[1]. The retentiveness of Socrates, however, could only have extended to the *enunciation* of decided views; as far as the mental act or judgment went, it seems more probable that his method was the effect of clearly-defined sentiments, which he thought could be more effectually inculcated by this indirect manner of teaching. "Il n'est pas croyable que Socrate ait vécu sans venir à bout de se persuader aucune verité, car il a mieux aimé mourir que se resoudre à conserver sa vie par des voyes qui ne lui paroîssoient point dans l'ordre. Peut-on reconnoître dans cette conduite le moindre caractère d'un esprit flôttant, et qui fait profession de ne pouvoir jamais distinguer surement *le Vrai* d'avec *le Faux*, et *le Juste* d'avec *l'Injuste*[2]?" The voluntariness or involuntariness of the state of mind which the ἐποχὴ indicated would *really* depend upon whether the arguments reviewed in support of any proposition were adscititious or adventitious; and it is more consistent with that general passivity characteristic of Pyrrhonism that reasons, the equal cogency of which induced the ἐποχὴ, were not sought after, but were forced on the attention of the post-Aristotelian Sceptics. The entire work of Sextus Empiricus is an evidence of this.

[1] M. Crousaz, *Examen du Pyrrhonisme*, Sect. II. VI. p. 17.
[2] *l. l.* p. 18.

The array of opposing dogmas exhibited in his treatise, comprising as it does every shade of philosophical or unphilosophical opinion, conjecture or belief, leaves us little room to wonder how those, who were at once learned and unprejudiced, found it impossible to feel assurance on any subject whatever. In truth, the Sceptic did not make the objections, but the objections made the Sceptic. M. Crousaz complains of the Sceptics, that their constant aim and object is to stifle every question with a mass of conflicting testimonies. But in reality the quibbles and sophistical shuffles, with which the work of Sextus Empiricus abounds, are arguments drawn from the opposing systems then prevalent, which cannot be laid to the account of the Pyrrhonists, inasmuch as they only availed themselves of materials found ready to their hands. Thus it was that the first trope of Agrippa could be applied in every branch of philosophical enquiry. Perhaps then the ἐποχή was the inevitable result of the dawn of science, when the shadows of poetical theogonies, supernatural agencies, and traditional superstitions, were beginning to disperse, but still obscured the paths to knowledge.

§ δ. There is no doubt that the ἐποχή, as a psychological phenomenon, was a result of the constitutional peculiarities of individuals, as well as of the circumstances of the age. To rest with the mind undetermined would argue either great indecision of character, or a restless hypercritical spirit, but certainly could not accompany a narrow or superficial understanding. The man who sees one idea to the exclusion of every other, or who reflects little, could not become a victim of the sceptical malady. It was quite natural then that the leaders of Pyrrhonism should have been men of great culture, and acute intellect; but for this very reason scepticism in its extreme form could never have been seriously maintained for any length of time. Accordingly we find it first tempered by Arcesilas, who maintained the *epoch* only in matters of speculative science; and subsequently more substantially modified by Carneades, and the later Academicians, by whom the indifference-point of scepticism was *past*, in three marked particulars. These constitute the basis of the distinction between the ultra-scepticism of the older Pyrrhonists and the more qualified form in which it was retained by the New Academy. The *epocha* then may be considered in some respects as the line of demarcation between Pyrrho and Carneades; and where the infraction of its reticence occurred the latter seems to have been considered by Sextus Empiricus to differ from the former. We have the main points of this distinction thus summed up in the *Hypotyposes*[1]. "The New Academicians differ from the Sceptics. 1. Inasmuch as they say all things are incomprehensible, for in this very affirmation, πάντα εἶναι ἀκατάληπτα, they assert something positively, whereas the Pyrrhonist does not despair of being able *eventually* perhaps to arrive at certainty, and the comprehension of things. 2. They differ from us more emphatically in their judgment concerning the good and the evil. For the Academicians pronounce things to be good or evil, not in the same sense as we do, but with the conviction it is more probable they are one rather than the other; whereas in our assertions about the good and the evil, we have no such conviction, but merely speak doubtfully, being forced to decide provisionally by the exigencies of life:—"ἡμῶν ἀγαθόν τι ἢ κακὸν εἶναι λεγόντων οὐδὲν μετὰ τοῦ πιθανὸν εἶναι νομίζειν ὃ φαμέν, ἀλλ' ἀδοξάστως ἑπομένων τῷ βίῳ, ἵνα μὴ ἀνενέργητοι ὦμέν." 3. *We* say that *all* our mental representations are equally trustworthy or untrustworthy, as materials for judgment. But *they* say some are probable, others improbable, and that there are degrees of probability. "τάς τε φαντασίας ἡμεῖς μὲν ἴσας λέγομεν εἶναι κατὰ πίστιν ἢ ἀπιστίαν, ὅσον ἐπὶ τῷ λογῷ, ἐκεῖνοι δὲ τὰς μὲν πιθανὰς εἶναι φασι, τὰς

[1] *Hyp.* 1. 33. 226.

δὲ ἀπιθάνους, καὶ τῶν πιθανῶν δὲ λέγουσι διαφοράς." This comparison, together with the exposition of the Academic doctrines to be found in the concluding chapters of *Lucullus*, enable us to estimate the essential distinction between the Pyrrhonian and Academic scepticism. The groundwork of this distinction, which was evidently detected by Sextus Empiricus himself, is, undoubtedly, the decision enunciated by the New Academicians concerning the relations of knowledge and objective reality. The fundamental problem of philosophy, viz. to distinguish the *thing* from the *appearance*, the *noumenon* from the *phenomenon*, the φαίνεσθαι ὄν from the φαίνεσθαι εἶναι, was abandoned as insoluble by the Academicians—for that is what we are to understand from the expression πάντα εἶναι ἀκατάληπτα—and in declaring the insolubility of this metaphysical problem, they separated themselves from the Pyrrhonists, in infringing the *epoch* by the decision itself, but most especially in completely altering the position of man in relation to metaphysical truth. Pyrrho is reported by Timon to have placed the knowledge of objective reality as a point of primary importance to man, δεῖν τὸν μέλλοντα εὐδαιμονήσειν εἰς τρία ταῦτα βλέπειν· πρῶτον μὲν, ὁποῖα πέφυκε τὰ πράγματα[1]. When then the New Academicians declared that our knowledge *did not*, and *never* could extend beyond phenomena, they virtually enunciated that the phenomenal apparent universe contained all that was of any interest to man. This declaration is remarkable, and indicates the close of an era in the history of philosophy. It separates metaphysic from physic by declaring the incomprehensibility of the former—it distinguishes speculative from practical knowledge, in that it resigns the hope of the former for ever. Here then we have the final decision of philosophy, confirming, however, only what Socrates had already announced, viz. that the enquiries into the ultimate causes,

[1] *Præparat. Ev.* xiv. 18 (Eusebius).

essences, or substantial existence of things, were beyond the grasp of human faculties. It was in the lingering adherence to the old fields of enquiry that Pyrrhonism found its most powerful incentive. The end pursued being unattainable, it was not difficult to challenge all endeavours to reach it. The Academicians not only resigned the chase, but implied that the happiness of life was alone dependent upon the relative and the phenomenal. It is thus that we interpret the *second* distinction taken by Sextus Empiricus between the Pyrrhonists and Academicians, viz. the positive decisions of the latter on the questions respecting the conduct of life. Man lives in a world of appearances, but on the relations of those appearances to himself and to each other depends everything which to a heathen philosopher constitutes happiness. Within this sphere then there is sufficient certitude upon which to ground principles of action. From observation and experience the good and the evil, or at any rate that which brought good and evil to man, could be determined; and it was absurd to maintain an attitude of suspense where the exigencies of life called for prompt decision. Hence arose that which has always been considered the distinguishing doctrine of the New Academy, namely—that a belief founded on *probable evidence* was sufficient ground of action for a reasonable being. This theory of probability seems principally to have been intended to meet a sceptical difficulty which had arisen in consequence of the confusion amongst early thinkers of the notions of *cognition* and *recognition*. The gist of this objection seems to have been—how can you *distinguish* one thing from another when you do not *know* either of them? It was to this quibble that the Academicians supplied the answer, that recognition only involved a comparison of appearances, and that these appearances might be taken as valid evidence in reference to each other. It was, indeed, not very philosophical of the Pyrrhonians to maintain that the mind had such a faculty of weighing evidence as to be able to detect its equivalence exactly, and yet not to admit that it was sometimes inclined in one direction more than another. Where there is the power of discerning equipollence there must also be the ability to perceive preponderance. It was true that recognition did not involve the assurance of that certainty which the Stoics imagined they had found in the cataleptic phantasm. Man might mistake Geminus, or fail to recognise Cotta; still, if the number of marks by which an object could be distinguished was observed with sufficient care, the degree of probability there would be that our judgment was right might amount to a virtual certainty. So the Academicians argued with equal cogency against the Stoics, who denied that they *ever* believed, and the Pyrrhonists, who denied that they *ever* could believe, or rather that the inconsistent beliefs destroyed each other. In opposing the special dogmas of the Stoics there is no doubt that Carneades far outstepped the reticence of the Pyrrhonian *epoch*, as in discussing the question of the criterion of truth. Still, as Cicero tells us, they retained an attitude of suspense in every science the premisses of which were incapable, or seemed incapable, of being established on any but probable evidence. As we said before, then, in matters of speculation the early Pyrrhonists and New Academicians may be said to have coincided in maintaining the ἐποχή; but in the affairs of practical life the latter declared a reasonable probability to be sufficient ground for action.

§ ε. With regard to the later development of Pyrrhonism, commenced by Ænesidemus soon after the death of Cicero, Brandis makes the following remarks[1]: "But in what consists the essential distinction between the Pyrrhonian and Academic scepticism? This is not easy to determine. They both disputed the possibility of knowing the nature of things,

[1] *Entwickelungen der Griechischen Phil.*, p. 230.

or of attaining any certitude whatever. They both allowed the facts of consciousness, and both aimed at the same end, viz. the enjoyment of a life undisturbed by knowledge, with its attendant hopes and fears, or by a useless struggle against the inevitable. But Carneades and the Academicians could not so far ignore the claims of science, as not to attempt a theory of probability; whereas Ænesidemus and his successors, convinced of the impracticability of such a theory, did not, like Antiochus the Academician, on this account give themselves up to a dogmatic eclecticism, but, without deserting the sceptical attitude, endeavoured to meet the emergencies of life, by observing the teachings of experience, by obeying the dictates of nature, by respecting laws and customs, and by acquiring useful arts. Remembered impressions—experience —appeared to belong to the phenomenal, for the images in memory could not be called in question, inasmuch as they were reproductions of appearances; especially as memory did not guarantee the causal dependence of events as necessary, but only suggested their possible recurrence in cases where absolute assurance was not required[1]. Similarly, the Sceptic might allow himself to be guided in his conduct by laws and customs, although he might neither approve of nor disallow them *per se*, and the inductions of experience he also admitted as a criterion of action. Opposition to established laws and customs, in fact, would have disturbed the tranquillity of his life; and he had no objection to avail himself of the experience of others[2]. For the same reason he did not hesitate to recognise piety as conducive to a peaceful existence[3]. The Sceptic substituted *empiricism* for *science*— which contented itself with meeting the requirements of life —which did not seek to discover the reality or ultimate causes of things, but merely observed the connexion of phe-

[1] *Adv. Math.* VIII. 291.   [2] *Hyp.* II. 256.
[3] *Hyp.* I. 24.

nomena, in order to be able to predict the future from a remembrance of the past, by virtue of the notion of causation, the natural attribute of humanity, without, however, committing himself to any decision respecting the reason of the thing. Hence Sextus Empiricus, in his discussion on the so-called five sciences, directs all his attacks against their theoretical principles, without in the least denying their utility for the purposes of life; but thinks they ought to be solely confined to practical limits, still with the consciousness that this restriction could seldom be strictly observed. So the Pyrrhonian scepticism allied itself to that which was in every case probable, and only attacked the theoretical part of science[1]."

§ ζ. We thus see that, as far as practical results went, the Sceptical Empiricism of the Academy, of which the final chapters of the *Lucullus* give us such a distinct picture, was adopted and maintained by the later representatives of Pyrrhonism. This accounts for the fact that Sextus Empiricus, although upholding the doctrines of Pyrrho, was in practical science a follower of the Empirical method. The extreme or earlier Pyrrhonism, he tells us[2], was only strictly adhered to by the so-called Methodists, who, with the Rationalists or Dogmatists and the Empirics, carried their respective philosophical opinions into the only art to which scientific principles were in those days applied, viz. that of Medicine. It is easy to see how well the Pyrrhonian or sceptical principles must have accorded with the circumstances of the times in which they were received. With the general collapse of the ancient national faith; with the universal corruption of morals; with a tyrannical government and a degenerate people; with just enough light in science to make darkness visible,

[1] *Adv. Math.* VII. 435.
[2] *Hyp.* I. 34. 236—241. Also, Note g, "Tria constat celebrari genera ac tres, veluti sectas medicorum," &c.

what could better correspond than a philosophical system which considered all religions as equally true, or equally false; which held the distinctions of good and evil to have no higher sanction than the arbitrary caprice, or hereditary tendencies of nations and individuals; which inculcated submission to the inevitable as a more certain means of ensuring tranquillity and happiness than brave and manly resistance; and which recognised in the human intellect no faculty of attaining to a knowledge of aught beyond the range of observation and experience? Wherever the features of scepticism are discernible they bear the stamp of despair, they indicate the close of a period in the world's history; they are the heralds of some mighty revolution in the moral, intellectual, and political relations of man. Such a revolution, we know, was even then in progress; and, at the time when Sextus Empiricus wrote, *must* already have attracted the attention of those who interested themselves in observing the varying phases of human development. It is then a question of some interest, why a philosopher with such a range of information, as the expounder of the sceptical doctrines evidently possessed, should have omitted even a passing notice of the Christian sect. It has, indeed, been supposed that he himself was a Christian, and the author of a book, mentioned by Eusebius, on the Resurrection[1]. Fabricius, it is true, does not seem to entertain this opinion; but, whether he was or was not a Christian himself, it is evident his silence concerning the new faith could not have arisen through ignorance. Perhaps respect for the pure lives and precepts of the Christians prevented him including them in the catalogue of heathen sects, of whose doctrines and manners he has only to relate something obscene and ridiculous[2]. Perhaps there was an element in scepticism favourable to Chris-

[1] *De Sexto Empirico, Testimonia* VII.
[2] *Hyp.* III. 24.

tianity, opposing as they both did, without reserve or exception, every form of heathen superstition. Paley, indeed, says, sceptics are not generally tolerant of a new religion. We doubt, however, whether this remark is applicable to the Pyrrhonian method. The Pyrrhonians only professed to suspend their judgment, declaring themselves perfectly willing to give their adherence to one opinion or another, the moment it could be made manifest to them that *any* given one was more worthy of credit than another. It is not probable, then, that a Pyrrhonian Sceptic would *primâ facie* reject any new doctrine, but rather be inclined to entertain it: not perhaps with much sincerity, but at least as affording additional justification for witholding his assent to any opinion whatever. Scepticism, under one form or another, was certainly the prevailing tone of Greek philosophy for three centuries before the commencement of the Christian era. We may be sure, then, that with the "increasing purpose, which through all ages runs," this tendency to invalidate all human attempts to attain the assurance of truth, was significant of the disclosure of a new faculty, which could be appealed to through some other avenue than that of the reason. "'We *know* (says St Austin) what rests upon *reason;* we *believe* what rests upon *authority.*' But reason itself must rest at last upon authority; for the original data of reason do not rest on reason, but are necessarily accepted by reason on the authority of what is beyond itself. These data are, therefore, in rigid propriety, Beliefs or Trusts[1]." Now it may seem at first sight paradoxical to assert that Pyrrhonism could in any way have been influential in guiding philosophers to the conviction that faith was the ultimate ground of reason; yet we think we can show that such a conclusion might result not illogically from the Sceptical habit of viewing things. We can illustrate what we mean by considering the force of that

[1] Reid's *Works* (Hamilton), Note A. § v. 2.

favourite weapon in controversy employed by the Sceptics, which we have had occasion more than once to notice, viz. the diallel. Of this logical net (M. Bayle says) "Si les Pirroniens s'aretôient aux dix moyens de l'Epoque, et s'ils se bornaient à les employer contre la Fisique, on pouroit encore négocier avec eux: mais ils vont beaucoup plus loin; ils ont une sort d'armes, qu'ils nomment le Dialléle, qu'ils empoignent au premier besoin, après cela on ne sauroit faire ferme contr'eux sur quoi que ce soit[1]." M. Bayle evidently regards the diallel as an arm against which reason was helpless. To what then did it reduce the adversary against whom it was employed? For example, suppose one asserted that the tree he was contemplating was really an external object, a *mode* of *matter*, and not a mere *idea, representation*, or *mode* of his own *mind*. The Sceptic would reply, Unless you have ever apprehended a tree, apart from your idea of it, how can you tell whether you are now contemplating an *object* in *reality*, or only an *idea* in the *mind?* you can only *know* the truth of your *idea* by the knowledge of the *object* of which it is the *idea;* but you can only *know* this *object* by the assurance you have of the truth of your *idea*. Here then are two things so related that you can alone establish the *first* by the *second*, and the *second* again by the *first;* thus you argue in a circle. But one might ask the Sceptic, Do you, in shewing the reciprocal dependence of the premise and conclusion of such an argument, make the belief of their actual existence absurd or impossible? It is clear that you do not; you merely fail to demonstrate either of them; you still leave it possible that they may be true; hence all you do is to throw me back on a principle of belief. The same consequence resulted from another of their logical meshes, viz. that of the proof regressing to infinity; for it is clear that, in this case also, the object was to drive the opponent back to some fundamental

[1] *Diction. Hist. et Crit.* (3 edit. Tom. III. p. 1005).

notion, or axiom, some instinctive belief. In fine, the sceptical method of arguing was, to force their adversary upon hypotheses; and it was then that the chief and most significant effect of their method of reasoning became apparent. The Sceptic did not refuse to admit first principles, incapable of demonstration; but he demanded that these principles should be consistent with one another, and lead to results which were so. It was here that scepticism could never be met, because philosophers either refused to recognise these *innate principles, à priori truths,* or *fundamental notions;* or they had destroyed the credibility of them *all* by refusing to admit *some.* In the former case, the diallel and the infinite regression obtained an easy victory; and in the latter, the Sceptic would urge with unanswerable justice, *I* accept the testimony of natural evidence; but, since *you* make it lead to opposing conclusions, *I still need* a criterion of truth. The point, however, we here want to establish is, that the pertinacious logic of the Sceptics must have forced the attention of philosophers to the nature of belief, and so have prepared the way, in some measure, for the acceptance of truths the most important to man, but which were, at the same time, incapable of demonstrative proof. We have seen that in the Academy the attempt to compass the objective reality of things was formally abandoned; but that belief, on probable evidence, was allowed as a practical principle in the affairs of life. Thus also in the scepticism of the Academy proof short of demonstrative was considered sufficient ground of action for a reasonable being. Hence, the influence of this school, as well as that of the Pyrrhonists, would be indirectly to accustom the philosophic mind to admit by faith that which could never become an object of knowledge. We should say then that the doctrines of Christianity probably found more adherents among the ranks of the sceptical than those of the dogmatic Empiricists. They, indeed, who held by the long-established conviction of the ancient sages, that the objective and the absolute were within the range of the human intellect, and who therefore aspired to the construction of a rational theology, sought refuge from scepticism in the mysticism of Plotinus and the Neo-Platonists. Thus faith, or reason, were each evoked as resting-ground from scepticism, on the quicksands of which the human mind could never find any permanent or solid satisfaction.

§ η. That the limits of knowledge prescribed by scepticism do not hinder the free exercise of faith, has been distinctly enunciated by the most orthodox theologians of the present day.

"Truth and falsehood are not properties of things in themselves, but of our conceptions, and are tested, not by the comparison of conceptions with things in themselves, but with things as they are given in some other relation. My conception of an object of sense is *true*, when it corresponds to the characteristics of the object as I perceive it; but the perception itself is equally a relation, and equally implies the co-operation of human faculties. Truth in relation to no intelligence is a contradiction in terms: our highest conception of absolute truth is that of truth in relation to all intelligences. But of the consciousness of intelligences different from our own we have no knowledge, and can make no application. Truth, therefore, in relation to man, admits of no other test than the harmonious consent of all human faculties[1]." There is not a statement in this passage which an ancient Sceptic would not have endorsed, and yet his very avowal of such opinions constituted his scepticism. For, allowing for the difference of language consequent upon the more philosophical distinctness of modern conceptions, what is there in this but an assertion that truth has for man no objective signification, but is limited to the relation of

[1] Mansel's *Bampton Lectures*, Lecture v. p. 149.

appearances, or of a subjective notion to an equally subjective perception? Truth not of what *is* but of what *appears* to be; not of the φαίνεσθαι ὂν, but of the φαίνεσθαι εἶναι; *internal* not *external* harmony. But still more striking is the accordance between ancient scepticism and modern orthodoxy in respect to the central notion of Pyrrhonism, viz. the relativity of all our knowledge; the τὸ πρός τι; the impossibility of separating subject and object even in thought. "A second characteristic of consciousness is, that it is only possible in the form of a *relation*. There must be a Subject, or person conscious, and an Object, or thing of which he is conscious. There can be no consciousness without the union of these two factors; and, in that union, each exists only as it is related to the other. The subject is a subject, only in so far as it is conscious of an object: the object is an object, only in so far as it is apprehended by a subject: and the destruction of either is the destruction of consciousness itself[1]." ὅτι δὲ καὶ πρός τι ἐστὶ πάντα τὰ αἰσθητὰ δῆλον· ἐστὶ γὰρ πρὸς τοὺς αἰσθανομένους. ἀλλὰ καὶ πρὸς τί ἐστὶ τὰ νοητὰ, πρὸς γὰρ τὸν νοοῦντα λέγεται[2]. Mansel even quotes Sextus Empiricus[3] in opposition to the German Absolutists, who seek to unite the subject and object as the only means of solving the logical difficulty of conceiving something out of relation to the thinking subject. The whole tenor, in fact, of Mansel's opinion coincides with that of ancient scepticism, much as the Oxford theologian might resent the imputation. In fact, both have the same end in view, to a certain extent, viz. the disparagement of the human reason; but ancient philosophers knew no faculty of belief in man which was not placed either in sense or in intellect, con-

---

[1] Mansel's *Bampton Lectures*, Lecture III. p. 75.
[2] *Hyp.* I. 15. 175—177.
[3] "Ὅλου δ' ὄντος τοῦ καταλαμβάνοντος οὐδὲν ἔτι ἔσται τὸ καταλαμβανόμενον τῶν δὲ ἀλογωτάτων ἐστὶ τὸ εἶναι μὲν τὸν καταλαμβάνοντα, μὴ εἶναι δὲ τὸ οὗ ἐστὶν ἡ κατάληψις."—*Adv. Math.* VII. 311.

sequently the Pyrrhonist, in demonstrating the feebleness of reason, destroyed all hope of attaining assurance. The Scoto-Oxonians have, however, devoted all their energies to the task of showing that we have an organ of faith independent of reason. It is a question whether, by adopting this method of defending their cause, they have met with the success they might have, had they taken up a rather different position. Sir W. Hamilton makes belief a mode of consciousness, and as such it necessarily implies a knowledge of its object. Professor Mansel, applying the principles of Hamilton to the discomfiture of the German rationalist theologians, endeavours to separate belief and knowledge, after setting out with the assumption that such a separation was impossible. Of course such a contradiction at the root of an argument would endanger the acceptance of the best cause. We think that the fundamental error of Hamilton and Mansel lies:

1st, in not distinguishing with sufficient clearness between the faculty and act of belief.

2nd, in making belief identical with feeling.

"I know it to be true, because I *feel* and cannot but *feel*," or "because I *believe* and cannot but *believe*, it so to be." And if farther interrogated, how I know or am assured that I thus *feel*, or thus *believe*, I can make no better answer than, in the one case, "because I *believe* that I *feel*," in the other, "because I *feel* that I *believe*[1]." But surely this is not a complete account of the kind of assent the mind gives to its natural testimony. The very notion of an *à priori* truth seems to us to be that the prejudice to accept it must be potentially in the mind, independent of the act which constitutes a belief identical with feeling; and this faculty, as distinguished from the act of belief, *might*, and in fact *does*, exist in the mind apart from reason, and exerts its influence without consciousness. Such is the belief the mind has in

[1] Reid's Works (Hamilton). Note A. § v. p. 760.

the validity of its own processes, which constitutes indeed the complement of the ultimate laws of thought. Belief then as a *faculty* or *potentiality* we might admit to be exercised on objects which could not be embraced by reason, but not as an *act* or *energy*. A nervous dread of German rationalism seems to have driven Dr Mansel to a denial of any relation between God and the human reason whatever; a degree of scepticism which might be more dangerous to orthodoxy than Teutonic mysticism.

§ θ. But to return to ancient scepticism: there is another aspect of the Hamiltonian philosophy, bringing it into a relation to early thought, which, as illustrative of our subject, demands some consideration. We have already noticed that a result of Pyrrhonism must have been to have forced philosophy into the admission of some ultimate principles innate in the human mind, as the sources and highest credentials of all our knowledge. In fact, the exaggerated empiricism of the Stoics was more than anything conducive to the spread of sceptical principles. Such a result we have also seen in the scepticism of Hume, which, following the empiricism of Locke, staggered the philosophical mind of Europe in the last century. The issue *involved* indeed in all the controversies between the ancient Dogmatists and Sceptics, but never *explicitly* stated, was forced into prominence by the subtle mind of Hume, when he shewed that the notion of causality, on which depends all our reasoning either moral, physical, or metaphysical, could not, on the hypothesis that the mind has no ideas but those derived from experience, be *demonstrated* to have any validity as a basis of argument. The dilemma into which he forced philosophers was really an example of the employment of the ancient diallel. No conviction is so universal, or so deeply seated in human intelligence, as that of the necessary connection between *cause* and *effect*, and no statement could consequently so tend to shake our faith in the testimony of consciousness as the announcement that this conviction was ill-grounded. "You say," said Hume "that we have no notions prior to experience, wherefore the idea of causation is only derived from experience, *i.e.* we trust to it because experience has always shown it to be worthy of confidence; but whence could this confidence have arisen if we had had no antecedent notion that the experience of the past was a guarantee in our anticipations of the future? Thus you affirm that we believe in *causation* from *experience*, and then say that we believe in *experience* through the notion of *causation;* here is a diallel. The notion of causation is therefore no necessary law of consciousness at all, but only the result of habit; and it is consequently no premiss to be assumed as fundamentally necessary; hence the testimony of consciousness, proved fallacious in one of its most undoubted deliverances, is not to be relied upon in any other—*false in one, false in all*[1]—scepticism could go no farther." The important bearing which the opinions of Hume had upon the interests of truth, subverting, as they appeared to do, the whole fabric of human knowledge, evoked the genius of Kant to undertake a searching investigation into the nature of our apprehensions of necessary and universal truths. It is doubtful whether the results of his critique of these notions much tended to re-establish faith in their objective validity, or whether he did not rather separate the spheres of the noumenal and phenomenal more irretrievably than ever. Even the controversy on the origin of our notions of mathematical and logical necessity seems as far from a satisfactory termination as ever. Dr Whewell (remarks Mansel[2]) in confounding the necessary laws under which all men think, with the contingent laws under which certain men think of certain things, seems to have given

---

[1] Hamilton's *Discussions. Philosophy of Perception*, p. 95.
[2] *Prolegomena Logica.* Note A.

some advantage to the empirical arguments of his antagonist Mr Mill. For Dr Whewell says of certain discoverers of physical laws: "So complete has been the victory of truth in most of these instances, that at present we can hardly imagine the struggle to have been necessary. The very essence of these triumphs is that they lead us to regard the views we reject as not only false, but inconceivable[1]." Of course to this Mr Mill could instantly reply: "The last proposition is precisely what I contend for; and I ask no more, in order to overthrow the whole theory of its author on the nature of the evidence of axioms. For what is that theory? That the truth of axioms cannot have been learnt from experience, because their falsity is inconceivable. But Dr Whewell himself says, that we are continually led, by the natural progress of thought, to regard as inconceivable what our forefathers not only conceived but believed, nay even (he might have added) were unable to conceive the reverse of[2]." We have quoted a fragment of this discussion in support of the assertion we just made, that the same questions which occupy modern thought were underlying the ancient antagonism of the Sceptics and Dogmatists. Thus we find Cicero (on behalf of the New Academy opposing the pretensions of Lucullus, who in the name of Antiochus is maintaining the claims to infallibility of the Stoics) noticing that tendency of the mind to assent unhesitatingly to certain propositions, continues: "Geometræ provideant (de persuadendi necessitate) qui se profitentur non persuadere, sed cogere: et qui omnia vobis, quæ describunt, probant. Non quæro ex his illa initia mathematicorum: quibus non concessis, digitum progredi non possunt. *Punctum* esse, quod magnitudinem nullam habeat. *Extremitatem*, et quasi libramentum, in quo nulla omnino crassitudo sit: *Lineam* autem, longitudinem latitu-

---

[1] *Phil. Ind. Sc.* II. 174.
[2] Mill's *Logic*, Book II. v. p. 273.

dine carentem. Hæc cum vera esse concessero : si adigam jusjurandum, sapientemne prius, quam Archimedes eo inspectante rationes omnes descripserit eas, quibus efficitur multis partibus solem majorem esse quam terram juraturum putas[1]." In this passage the distinction between objective and subjective laws seems to have been unconsciously recognised (if we may use the expression), and might warrant us in the conclusion that certain principles of reasoning were left unassailed by the Sceptics. It is true that Galen asserts Carneades denied the truth of the maxim, 'things which are equal to the same are equal to one another:' "ὁ γοῦν Καρνεάδης οὐδὲ τοῦτο τὸ πάντων ἐναργέστατον συγχωρεῖ πιστεύειν, ὅτι τὰ τῷ αὐτῷ ἴσα μεγέθη καὶ ἀλλήλοις ἴσα γίγνεται[2]."

Brandis thinks[3] this refers to the application of the axiom to the prosecution of real knowledge owing to the uncertainty of the senses. We are inclined to think, however, all that Carneades meant was, that such a truth was not a generalisation from experience; and in this he probably was only maintaining the traditions of the Academy. The fact of the universal belief in such a proposition he certainly could not have challenged. Perhaps here again we have the scepticism of Hume anticipated. However uncertain we may be about the opinions of the New Academy respecting first principles, Sextus Empiricus, on behalf of the Pyrrhonists, enunciates them continually, as the basis of all reasoning. Thus, arguing on the impossibility of demonstration, he urges that there is a class of truths indemonstrable, because they are self-evident: "τῶν ὄντων πᾶσι φαινομένων ἐπ' ἴσης ἔσται ἀδίδακτα[4]." Just as Aristotle defines an axiom

[1] Lucullus, 86.   [2] Galen, de Opt. Doctr. c. 2. p. 45.
[3] "Carneades scheint daraus die praktische Unanwendbarkeit des Satzes gefolgert zu haben, das zwei Grössen die einer dritten gleich, auch unter einander gleich seien."—Brandis, Enwickelungen der Griechischen Phil. p. 187, Note 50.
[4] Adv. Math. I. 2. 14.

to be, "that, which he who would learn aught, must himself bring, and not receive from his instructor." And in the exordium to his work against logicians, Sextus Empiricus says, "ὡς εἴπερ ἐν παντὶ μέρει φιλοσοφίας ζητητέον ἐστὶ τἀληθές, πρὸ παντὸς δεῖ τὰς ἀρχὰς καὶ τοὺς τρόπους τῆς τούτου διαγνώσεως ἔχειν πιστούς:—ἐπεὶ τὰ μὲν ἐναργῆ διὰ κριτηρίου τινὸς αὐτόθεν γνωρίζεσθαι δοκεῖ, τὰ δὲ ἄδηλα διὰ σημείων καὶ ἀποδείξεων κατὰ τὴν ἀπὸ τῶν ἐναργῶν μετάβασιν ἐξιχνεύεσθαι[1]." As we remarked before, Pyrrhonism never refused the admission of primary truths, but founded exclusively on their apparent contradiction. The universal beliefs of mankind were undoubtedly criteria of truth to the Sceptic[2]; and his very scepticism arose from his professed inability to discover such beliefs common to the human race. There are no truths, says he, moral or physical, because that which is true would appear so to all. Such is the reiteration of the Pyrrhonist: "That which is true would appear so to all, but *nothing* does appear so to all, therefore *nothing* is true." Scepticism, therefore, "en dernière analyse," really acknowledged a criterion of truth, viz. "the common beliefs of mankind." Philosophy had subverted these beliefs; and it was quite competent then for the Sceptic to demand of philosophy a new criterion in place of the one she had disallowed. Such was the real attitude of scepticism in relation to dogmatic philosophy, when stripped of the exaggerations of its own professors, and the misrepresentations and misapprehensions of its adversaries. On this ground alone can scepticism be fairly met and confuted. It would be a task of much interest and of great importance to the cause of philosophy to investigate when and how the schism between philosophy and common

---

[1] *Adv. Logicos*, VII. 24. 25.

[2] Cf. "ὁ γὰρ πᾶσι δοκεῖ, τοῦτ' εἶναι φαμέν. ὁ δ' ἀναιρῶν ταύτην τὴν πίστιν οὐ πάνυ πιστότερα ἐρεῖ."—Aristotle, *Eth. Nic.* K. 2. 4.

"καθὼς ὁ Τίμων μεμαρτύρηκεν εἰπών, ἀλλὰ τὸ φαινόμενον παντὶ σθένει, οὗπερ ἂν ἔλθῃ."—*Adv. Logicos*, VII. 30.

sense first originated. Scepticism is not a natural product of the human mind, at least, as far as regards the testimony of consciousness. It is an universally admitted characteristic of children and barbarians, that they believe implicitly until their natural faith has been shaken by some extraneous cause; and the stronger the instinctive belief has been, the more difficult would it be to restore it when once impaired. It was on this account that the writings of Hume created such an effect on the minds of philosophers. In the infancy of Greek speculation such an advanced scepticism as that of Hume was hardly likely to have appeared. But there are beliefs common to the human race, and as unhesitatingly accepted by the natural mind as the belief in causation. To the undermining of these, Greek scepticism owed its origin. To illustrate our meaning we will quote the following passage from Eusebius: "It is worth while to enquire on what authority they (the Pyrrhonists) say, that everything is hidden (ἄδηλα); for they ought to be able to determine the evident (τὸ δῆλον), then they would be competent to declare what things are not evident. One ought to know the affirmative, before one can state the negative. If they do not know what is evident, they will not know what is non-evident. Thus, when Enesidemus in his Hypotyposes instituted his nine τρόποι, by which he tried to show that everything is uncertain (ἄδηλα), let us ask whether he did it *knowing* them or not. For he says that animals differ, and we ourselves, and cities, habits, customs, and laws; that our senses are weak, and that external circumstances hinder our knowledge, such as distance, size, and motion. That the young feel differently to the old, the waking to the sleeping, the healthy to the sick. That nothing we apprehend is absolute or simple (ἀκραιφνές), that all things are relative and complex. I say he talks nonsense, for some one would instantly enquire, does he affirm these things *knowing* how far they are so, or not *knowing* it. If he did not know, how should we believe him; but if he knew it, he would be a fool, inasmuch as he at the same time says that he *knows* these things, and yet declares that everything is *hidden*[1]." In this argumentation, it would appear that the philosopher sought to force the Sceptic into a self-contradiction; "how do you know *everything* is *hidden,* and yet know *nothing?*" but, to this the Sceptic might reply, I should not have known that all things were hidden, unless your philosophy had suggested such a conclusion. "Democritus (says Sir W. Hamilton) was the first who enounced the observation, that the Sweet, the Bitter, the Cold, the Hot, the Coloured, &c. are wholly different, in their absolute nature, from the character in which they become manifested to us[2]." Now, if this was the case, Democritus was the first who discovered to man a faculty of separating the *appearance* from the *thing,* the *apparent* from the real, the φαίνεσθαι εἶναι from the φαίνεσθαι ὄν; and, in endowing man with this faculty, Democritus lent to him a real basis for the art of doubting; and we are not surprised to read that it was the perusal of the works of Democritus which first suggested to Pyrrho the notion of systematising scepticism into a method of philosophy. "Men are carried away by a natural instinct to repose faith in their senses. When they follow this blind and powerful instinct of nature, they always suppose the *very images* presented to the senses *to be* the external objects, and never entertain any suspicion that the *one* are nothing but representations of the *other*[3]." But once shake this faith, once demonstrate to man, that the testimony of his consciousness (than which

[1] *Præparat. Ev.* xiv. 18.
[2] Reid's Works. Hamilton. Note D. § 1.
[3] Hume, *Phil. Works,* Vol. iv. p. 177.

nothing *primâ facie* is more certain) is a fallacy and a delusion, then you cannot deny to scepticism a valid and plausible ground of argument. Philosophers are (as Hume states) thrown upon this dilemma: "Do you, he asks (firstly), follow the instinct and propensities of nature in assenting to the veracity of sense? But these lead you to believe that the *very perception*, or *sensible image*, is the *external object*." (Thus secondly), "Do you *disclaim* this *principle* in order to embrace a more rational opinion, that the perceptions are only *representations* of something external? You here depart from your natural propensities, and more obvious sentiments, and yet are not able to satisfy your reason, which can never find any convincing argument from experience to prove that the perceptions are connected with any external objects." And we maintain that a careful examination of the principles of Pyrrhonism cannot but lead to the conviction, *that* it was on this false theory of perception, which, in one form or another, seems to have been universally accepted by ancient thinkers, that scepticism grew and fattened. "Plato's theory of perception is that denoted by some modern writers as the 'representative theory.' Of things as they are in themselves the *senses* give us no knowledge: all that in sensation we are conscious of is a state of mind or feeling (πάθος); the existence of self or the perceiving subject, and of a something external to self—a perceived object—are revealed to us, not by the senses, but by a higher faculty. The *negative* portion of this theory Plato holds in common with the Cyrenaics, with Protagoras, and with the later Academics and Sceptics. It was controverted by the Stoics, who maintained that the external world is the object of *immediate* consciousness (καταληπτόν). But all the remaining schools of antiquity,—sceptical, dogmatic, and mystical,—agree with Plato in denying that our sensations reveal to us anything beyond themselves. They are modifications of consciousness, feelings, states,—*permotiones intimæ* (as Cicero has it),—and *nothing more*[1]."

This account of the opinions generally held by ancient thinkers on the degree of knowledge we have of the external universe leads us to assert that Greek scepticism was mainly determined by a mistaken view of the real object apprehended in perception. To whatever results an habitual methodical unbelief may have led, however deplorable they may have been, and subversive of all immutable principles of morality, still it is not through and on account of these results that scepticism is to be met and refuted;—it is the principles, and not their consequences, that ought fairly to be attacked, and for these, as we think, we have shewn not scepticism but philosophy is responsible. Scepticism, both ancient and modern, has never and could never have been an independent manifestation of human opinion, but wherever it has appeared it has been due to an erroneous method of philosophising.

Sir William Hamilton detecting this, made it the principal end of his teaching to reconcile the conflicting judgments of philosophy and common sense, on this much vexed question of the nature of our perceptions, in order to remove the contradictions which Hume showed must inevitably arise from according belief to some of the deliverances of consciousness and withholding it from others. Locke had articulately enunciated a distinction which he considered

---

[1] Dr Thompson's note to Butler's *Lectures*, Lecture VII. p. 96. Tennemann seems to think that Pla o considered a knowledge of the subject to be involved in the act of perception: "Dass mit jeder Vorstellung ein Bewustsein verbunden ist, war ein Faktum, das sich jedem Beobachter von selbst aufdringet; und es wäre eine Art von Wunder, wenn sie dem Plato entgangen wäre. Man findet zwar dieses Faktum in seiner Allgemeinheit und mit bestimmten Worten ausgedruckt nicht in seinen Schriften erwähnt, aber doch einzelne Bermerkungen und Aeusserungen, aus welchen so viel erhellet, dass es ihm nicht unbekannt geblieben war."—Tennemann's *Platonischen Philosophie*, zweiter Band, Kap. 1. p. 13.

must be taken between the primary and secondary qualities of external objects. Of the latter he asserted we only had a mediate and relative knowledge as the *unknown causes* of certain modifications of consciousness, or ideas, as he termed them;—that our apprehensions of colour, taste, and smell were but knowledge of changes in the percipient subject, ideas which resembled nothing external to the mind. Of *primary* qualities, such as extension, figure, solidity, &c. he maintained we had a distinct and quasi-immediate cognition, or, what amounts to the same thing, that our ideas of them did resemble their cause in nature. It was not long after Locke had published his celebrated work, that Berkeley completed the idealism of Locke by demonstrating that the so-called *primary qualities* were no more the objects of immediate perception than the *secondary*. That in fact all we could assert of things apparently external was our act of perceiving them; their *esse* is *percipi*. Although this doctrine was carried by him, or rather carried him, to some very extravagant conclusions, there is no doubt that this placing of the primary and secondary qualities of bodies on the same footing, as phenomena of consciousness, was a conclusion of the last importance to the interests of philosophy; and if regarded from a right point of view, the most substantial bulwark against the encroachments of scepticism. Unfortunately, however, the idealistic tendency which philosophy had received from the writings of Locke caused the opinions of Berkeley respecting the primary and secondary qualities of bodies to have an exactly opposite effect. Scepticism in its subtlest form broke out, and, as we have already seen, Hume challenged philosophers on their ideal theory of perception to demonstrate logically, the existence of any external world at all. It was then that Reid attempted to meet scepticism by an appeal to the common sense or common beliefs of mankind, which, as an ultimate criterion of truth, he invoked against the assaults of the sceptic. For this purpose Reid, while for ever annihilating a capital error, vitiating up to his time all speculation (viz. the separation of the *act* from the *object* of perception), revived Locke's distinction between the primary and secondary qualities; maintaining that our knowledge of the *former* was intuitive—an universal belief of mankind, and a sufficient proof of the existence of an external and extended universe. With regard to secondary qualities, however, he held to the opinion of philosophy, and at the same time appeared to hold it doubtful whether philosophers and the vulgar really differed concerning them. "We are now (says he) to consider the opinions both of the vulgar and of philosophers upon this subject. As to the former, it is not to be expected that they should make distinctions which have no connection with the common affairs of life; they do not, therefore, distinguish the primary from the secondary qualities, but speak of both as being equally qualities of the external object. Of the primary qualities they have a distinct notion, as they are immediately and distinctly perceived by the senses; of the secondary, their notions, as I apprehend, are confused and indistinct, rather than erroneous. A secondary quality is the unknown cause or occasion of a well-known effect; and the same name is common to the cause and the effect. Now, to distinguish clearly the different ingredients of a complex notion, and at the same time the different meanings of an ambiguous word, is the work of a philosopher, and is not to be expected of the vulgar, when their occasions do not require it. I grant, therefore, that the notion the vulgar have of secondary qualities is indistinct and inaccurate. But there seems to be a contradiction between the vulgar and the philosopher upon this subject, and each charges the other with a gross absurdity. The vulgar say, that fire is hot, and snow cold, and sugar sweet; and that to deny this is a gross absurdity, and contradicts the testimony of our senses. The philosopher says that heat, and cold, and sweetness are nothing but sensations in our minds, and it is absurd to conceive that these sensations are in the fire, or in the snow, or in the sugar. The philosopher says, there is no heat in the fire, meaning that the fire has not the sensation of heat. His meaning is just; and the vulgar will agree with him, as soon as they understand his meaning. But his language is improper; for there is really a quality in the fire, of which the proper name is heat; and the name of heat is given to this quality, both by philosophers and by the vulgar, much more frequently than to the sensation of heat[1]." Upon this account of the natural beliefs of man as to what they are actually conscious of in perception, Sir W. Hamilton grounds his doctrine of Natural Realism, which proclaims, that that which in the act of perception is presented to us as an external extended substance, is really the external extended substance, and not a mere representation of it—a real mode of matter, and not a mere mode of mind; and thus, he maintains, and only thus, is it possible to controvert the sceptical dilemma by which philosophy is made to stultify itself by first wresting from man one of his most cherished and universal beliefs, and then appealing to the same belief as a certain evidence of the existence of external objects. Now the whole value of the service Sir W. Hamilton has rendered to philosophy must evidently depend upon the fact whether or not the doctrine he upholds is one in accordance with the universal belief of mankind. For the object he professedly has in view is to shew that these beliefs are the ultimate criteria of truth; and it is only in deserting them that philosophy has laid herself open to the attacks of Scepticism. Now, we reply, that, so far from the

---

[1] *On the Int. Powers*, II, XVII. 241.

testimony of consciousness revealing to us any distinction between the primary and secondary qualities of matter, the maintenance of this distinction would cause *that very conflict which*, as Sir W. Hamilton admits, is and always has been the prime cause of scepticism.

The natural and universal belief of mankind is certainly that, in the act of perception, one is conscious of an *ego*, and a *non-ego*—of oneself as subject perceiving, and of a not-self as object perceived: and it is the changes in this object, as modes of *matter*, not modes of *mind*, which constitute for man the materials of his consciousness. He makes, however, no distinction between his apprehensions of colour, fragrance, figure, or solidity; all are alike to him qualities of the object, as Reid, in fact, in the first part of our quotation admits. Heat, cold, and such subjective sensations, man apprehends not as modifications of his own mind, but as changes in his body. These changes are perceived as the effects from objects external to the body, which are causes; and when we speak of the qualities of external objects, as heat in the fire, we regard them as the causes of changes in our own bodies, and they correspond to those powers or qualities which Locke calls the *tertiary* qualities, and James Mill the *causes* of the *causes* of our sensations. Sir William Hamilton admits that it is absurd to ask how the *ego* can be conscious of the *non-ego*, unless it can be shewn how it can be conscious of changes in itself. As far as the so-called *primary* qualities go, he would have us believe that we perceive changes in matter, or in the *non-ego;* but, with regard to the *secondary*, they are changes in the percipient mind. As we have said, the vulgar do not make this distinction, but regard all their perceptions as apprehensions of changes in matter. Sir W. Hamilton says, Common sense does not mean the opinion of the vulgar, but those ultimate principles of belief which are to be discriminated by the philosopher. Let us turn then from the opinions of the vulgar to those of philosophers.

There are certain laws of thought which would prevent us logically from allowing any difference between *primary* and *secondary* qualities of matter. "All the secondary qualities may be generalized at one sweep into *our mere* knowledge of things. But the primary qualities—which are usually restricted to extension and figure, and which constitute, it is said, the objective or real essence of things, and which are entirely independent of us—into what shall they be generalized? Into what but into this? Into the *knowledge* of something which exists in things over and above *our mere* knowledge of things. It is plain enough that we cannot generalize them into pure objective existence in itself; we can only generalize them into a *knowledge* of pure objective existence. But such a knowledge, that is to say, a knowledge of something existing in things, over and above our *mere* knowledge of them, is not one whit less *our* knowledge, and is not one whit more *their* existence, than the other more subjective knowledge designated by the word *mere*. Our knowledge of extension and figure is just as little these real qualities themselves as our affection of colour is objective colour itself. Just as little, we say, and just as much. You (we suppose ourselves addressing an imaginary antagonist), you hold that our knowledge of the secondary qualities is not these qualities themselves; but we ask you, Is then our knowledge of the primary qualities these qualities themselves? This you will scarcely maintain, but perhaps you will say, Take away the affection of colour, and the colour no longer exists; and we retort upon you, Take away the knowledge of extension, and the extension no longer exists. This you will peremptorily deny, and we deny it just as peremptorily; but why do both of us deny it? Just because both of us have surreptitiously restored the knowledge of extension in denying that extension itself would be annihilated. The knowledge of extension *is* extension, and extension *is* the knowledge of extension[1]."

Such are the arguments by which a distinguished metaphysician of the present age has, as we think, irrefutably demonstrated the impossibility of separating the primary and secondary qualities of bodies in consciousness. We do not say we are prepared to subscribe to the ultra-idealism, or rather Berkleyism, which his philosophy implies; but we maintain, that to distinguish our knowledge of the external universe into two kinds, *is* to endow man with a putative faculty which nature has not given him, by which he is induced to separate the apparent from the real, and thus institute a discrepancy in the testimony of consciousness, which, as Hamilton has laboured with so much earnestness to show, is the one and only means by which this testimony could be invalidated. Positivism and empiricism are at the present day the popular tendencies of thought.

Induction is the only method of attaining knowledge; and *à priori* principles, on the existence of which the whole validity of induction depends, the ablest supporters of this method refuse to admit. It becomes then the duty of philosophers to unite in defence of such principles as the only barrier against scepticism. Let the instinctive beliefs of mankind, discriminated and interpreted, be accepted as the ultimate criteria of truth. But, above all, let philosophers take care to maintain the integrity of their testimony. The philosopher's infirmity is the sceptic's opportunity.

[1] Ferrier, *Berkeley and Idealism*, p. 317.

APPENDIX A.

NOTES FOR LECTURES ON CICERO'S LUCULLUS.

(TEXT, EDITION OF KLOTZ.)

CHAP. I. 2. *artem ei memoriæ quæ tum primum proferebatur*] The Sophists were probably the first who attempted to cultivate the memory by artificial means. Such proficiency was an indispensable accessory to rhetorical art. Aristotle has left us the best and most pregnant essay on memory (*De Memoria*), in which the phenomenon is carefully analysed, the laws of the association of ideas indicated, and the nature of the mental image precisely defined. The notice of the faculty of memory in the exordium to this work is remarkably relevant, since it was really the only power the Stoics allowed to the mind. See Chapters VII. 22, memoriae quidem, &c., x. 30, XXXIII. 106.

II. 4. *Quum autem e philosophis ingenio scientiaque putaretur Antiochus, Philonis auditor excellere*, &c.] See Lecture V. § *a*, ibid. § ζ.——7. *Sunt etiam qui negent*, &c.] Cicero was evidently brought to the same opinion ultimately. Hence the recall of the first edition of this work. See Lecture I. p. 20, note 2.

III. 7. *Restat unum genus*, &c.] The Dogmatists, i.e. the Stoics, Epicureans, and Peripatetics. These, with the Academicians (Sceptics) divided between them the domain of Greek Philosophy during the three centuries preceding the Christian Era.

Sextus Empiricus opens his review of the doctrines of the Sceptics with the following leading distinctions among philosophers: 'They who seek for anything (says he) must either have found it, or admit that it is not to be found, or, finally, uncertain whether it is to be found or not persevere still in the search.' So it is with the questions of Philosophy. One sect say they have discovered the truth, a second that it is unattainable, and a third continue its pursuit. The first are the Dogmatists; the second, Carneades, Clitomachus, and the Academicians; the third, the Sceptics. In this description a distinction is made between the Academicians and Sceptics which is unreal; or, rather, it applies to the end and not to the method of Philosophy.——*ratio non probatur*] The proper translation of *ratio* is method, i.e. any road, way, or means to an end in the field of knowledge or philosophy the end is truth; the method or means to that end is evidence; hence method in its philosophical signification is the theory of evidence (logic) as understood by Mr Mill. The Dogmatists and Sceptics then differed concerning the theory of evidence or means of discovering truth. In this controversy the Academicians were certainly Sceptics. But the truth indicated in this passage from Sextus E. is what we understand now as metaphysical or ontological truth; that is, the reality of things *per se*. This, the Academicians, anticipating the decision of Kant, resigned as unattainable. The Dogmatists, considering all truth to be bound up with the real nature and essence of things, confused metaphysical and physical enquiries, never distinctly separated until the present day.——*Nos autem*] Cicero here proclaims himself as belonging to the school of the Academy. Only in metaphysical speculations, however, for in moral philosophy he must be classed with the Stoics. He was more properly an eclectic.——*eliciant et tamquam exprimant*] The cross-examining, maieutic method or dialectic of Socrates is here alluded to. It was the characteristic manner of the Academy to discover truth by questioning man, in whom, according to the philosophy of Socrates and Plato, the *first principles* of knowledge were latent. Socrates adopted a *pseudo-inductive* method for eliciting these principles; i.e. he endeavoured to eliminate conflicting opinions, δόξαι, from the genuine ἐπιστήμη. It was Bacon who first announced the fertile observation that to arrive at knowledge it was necessary to question nature, not man.

IV. 10. *Etsi heri, inquit*] The nature of the preceding discussion is betrayed by the following references: VI. 18, jam enim

hoc pro φαντασίᾳ verbum satis hesterno sermone trivimus; XIII.
42, XVI. 49, XVIII. 59, XXV. 79.——*non vinci me malim quam
vincere*] This is a Socratic adage, as in the Gorgias Socrates tells
his interlocutor he would rather be refuted than himself refute.
——11. *in ista philosophia*] That of the Academy. Clitomachus
was the pupil and mouthpiece of Carneades, the third leader of
the Academy; Philo was the fourth, Antiochus the fifth, who
coalesced the opinions of the Academy with those of the Stoa;
hence was in opposition to Carneades and Philo. The doctrines
of the Academy were revived again by the later Pyrrhonists
under Æaesidemus.——12. *contra suum doctorem*] Thus Antiochus
ranged himself in direct antagonism to Philo and Carneades.——
Ad Arcesilam] the second leader of the Academy. Thus the five
chief men were Plato, Arcesilas, Carneades, Philo, and Antiochus.

V. 13. *me autem*] Cicero—the two interlocutors therefore
are Cicero speaking as and for the Academy against Lucullus
personating Antiochus, who had deserted the Academy for the
Stoa; therefore is attacking the Academy with all the hostility
of a renegade.——*veteres physicos*] It is a common habit with the
upholders of certain opinions to maintain that the same doctrines
have been held by every one else. So the Sceptics tried to show
that all former philosophers had been Sceptics likewise (cf. Diog.
L. IX.). The Pre-Socratic philosophers were called physical
because their enquiries were chiefly concerning φύσις, or the real
nature of things. They would now be called metaphysical or
ontological speculatists.——15. *Peripateticos et Academicos, nominibus differentes, re congruentes*] It has been a prevalent opinion
that there were antithetical distinctions between Plato and
Aristotle. Every man it is said is born either a Platonist or an
Aristotelian. Sometimes Plato is considered an Idealist, Aristotle
a Materialist. Plato is often held to have depended on *à priori*
or intuitive principles of knowledge, whilst Aristotle was an
Empiricist, or one who derived all knowledge *à posteriori* from
experience. We have not space here to refute these erroneous
views, but recommend the student to adopt the opinion expressed
in the text, trusting to his own reading for confirmation of it.

VI. 17. *ullam rationem*] We have said above (III. 7) that
ratio means method, and that method is the way to truth, i.e.
evidence. How evidence is to be collected, estimated, verified

and applied, is method.—Now the Academicians challenged the validity of evidence altogether. With what evidence, therefore, was it possible to meet them? We may consider the subject-matter of the following discussion to be the *evidentness of evidence*. An illustration will place the dispute in a clear light. A witness gives his evidence in a court of justice; it is manifest the value of his evidence must in a great measure depend upon his veracity. This can be attacked, and requires evidence to support it—this second evidence may again have to be based on other evidence, and so *ad infinitum*. Now the Stoics maintained that there was a kind of evidence whose evidentness was in itself and shone as it were by its own light. Such evidence they called κατάληψις (cognitio aut perceptio aut......comprehensio, quam κατάληψιν illi vocant). For the origin of the term κατάληψις, see Ch. XLVII. 145. Also Lect. IV. § β. The Academicians held that such self-evident evidence was impossible. The instance which is to be taken in the following treatise, and which in fact afforded a capital opportunity for each side to try the temper of their weapons, was the phenomena of external perception. Here the nature of evidence could be tested in its simplest, most general, and most important applications. The student must not be repelled by the apparent puerility of many of the arguments;—the *evidentness* of *evidence* is one of the most momentous questions for man to decide upon, and, although human beings can get on very well with the unsupported evidence of their senses, yet the greatest philosophers of every age have made the theory of perception the basis of all psychological, logical and metaphysical enquiries.——
eosque, qui persuadere vellent......aut evidentiam nos] The student must attend particularly to this passage, the meaning of which is that the Academicians would not admit the evidentness of any evidence. It is therefore no use trying to convince them by persuasion, argument, or evidence, because the process would be interminable.
——*sed tamen orationem nullam putabant illustriorem ipsa evidentia reperiri posse*] Translate *orationem*, argument.——18. *id enim volumus esse ἀκατάληπτον*] This doctrine of ἀκατάληπτον or incomprehensibility simply denied the evidentness of any evidence whatever. The counter-doctrine was illustrated by Zeno the founder of the Stoics through the φαντασία or *visum*, i.e. the change of consciousness in the individual through which as an

effect, *impressum effictumque*, any external object betrays its presence as causes. Now on what evidence do we say a white object is white? surely, this is a case of *self-evident evidence* where belief is compelled. The sceptical reply to this instance we have dwelt upon with sufficient length in Lecture III. § a. The whiteness in consciousness is only *self-evident evidence* of itself. Its cause or the external object may produce in another person a different consciousness—or it may be excited by a nervous disorder (See Lect. IV. note 1, page 73). So far from being a capital instance of *self-evident evidence* it is merely a proof of the fallibility of every kind of evidence.

There is an anacoluthon in the paragraph *id enim volumus esse ἀκατάληπτον,—si illud esset, sicut Zeno definiret, tale visum— jam enim hoc pro φαντασίᾳ verbum satis hesterno sermone trivimus ......visum igitur impressum effictumque ex eo unde esset, quale esset non posset, ex eo, unde non esset.*—First, *illud* refers to ἀκατάληπτον, then is apposed by *tale visum*, then the sentence is broken and the *visum* afterwards described is a perception impressed on the mind by such a cause or external object as could not but produce it, i.e. the effect could only have but one cause; now the ἀκατάληπτον is the exact opposite of this. The anacoluthon may be avoided by omitting the *non* in the sentence *quale esse non posset;* in this case it will not be the visum which is defined, but the ἀκατάληπτον *visum.——Quo minime vult, revolvitur*] The vicious circle in which it is sought to involve Philo is, that if, as he said, *all* evidence rests on other evidence, upon what does he Philo rest the evidence of this assertion?

VII. 19. *remo inflexo aut de collo columbæ*] See Lecture III. page 49—infra ch. xxx. Favourite illustration with the Sceptics of the fallibility of the senses. A stick in the water appears bent when it is really straight.

"Law is God, say some; no God at all, says the fool;
For all we have power to see is a straight staff bent in a pool."

Epicurus hoc viderit et alia multa] Cf. xxv. 79; xxxii. 101. The Epicureans or Epicurus thought that perception was caused by an object throwing off a sort of filmy image of itself which impinged on the senses and was an *exact* representation of the object from which it proceeded. Thus in vision they held it absurd to say the sun or moon were any larger than they appeared to be.——*si et sani sunt*] This is begging the question altogether; as Cicero's object is to upset the arguments of the Stoics maintained by Lucullus, he would naturally not establish them on too firm a basis. For an exposition of the entire subject, see Lectures III. and IV., especially the note from Mill's Logic, Lect. IV. page 73. Most of our judgments through the senses are not simple judgments; they are inferences, as the student will there see.——*Quod idem fit in vocibus*, &c.] See Bain, *On the Senses and Intellect*, Book II. ch. 2. The power of discriminating differences and detecting resemblances is the ultimate fact of consciousness, the basis of all intelligence.——20. *Cyrenaici*] The followers of Aristippus; they held that the distinctions of pleasure and pain were the only immediate judgments which did not involve an inference. *This is pleasant to me* is a judgment about that which philosophers term a *subjective* fact; it cannot be gainsayed, it requires no proof, and is therefore not an inference; but the judgment *this is white* (21. illud est album, hoc dulce) is by no means on the same footing, i.e. if by *this* I mean some external object the permanent cause of a constant effect called whiteness, because the *same* object will often not produce the *same* effect. The ratiocination accompanying such a perception would be, *whatever* appears *white* is *white*, this object appears *white*, therefore we have the inference this object *is white*. Here the Sceptics attack the major premiss allowing only the minor; see Sextus Empiricus, *Hyp.* I. 10, 19, 20, also Lect. III. § β.

"We do not arraign the passive representations of consciousness, τὰ κατὰ φαντασίαν παθητικά. For they compel our assent involuntarily, inasmuch as they are phenomena. But, when we come to enquire whether the external object (τὸ ὑποκείμενον) is such as it appears to be, we admit there is no question about the phenomenon, but about that which is *inferred* from the phenomenon, περὶ ἐκείνου ὃ λέγεται περὶ τοῦ φαινομένου. For example, 'honey tastes sweet;' so much we allow, for we are conscious of the taste through a direct sensation, γλυκαζόμεθα γὰρ αἰσθητικῶς. But we doubt whether we are justified in passing the judgment '*this is sweet*,' for that is not the phenomenon, but something asserted concerning the phenomenon. ὃ οὐκ ἔστι τὸ φαινόμενον, ἀλλὰ περὶ τοῦ φαινομένου λεγόμενον.——21. *Animo jam hæc tenemus comprehensa, non sensibus*] The meaning of this is, before we can recognise an object as white, we must have a clear idea of what whiteness is. This will apply equally to any judgment even the most subjective—we cannot say this is pleasure unless we have a general idea of pleasure already in the mind. Hence the formation of conceptions or general notions is always considered the first step in the acquisition of knowledge. Mr Mill, however, controverts this opinion (see Mill's *Logic*, I. ch. v.). '*Ille*' *deinceps* '*equus est, ille canis.*'] See note from Mill's *Logic*, Lect. IV. p. 73 and Lect. V.——22. ἔννοίας.] See Lecture IV. § a, p. 66, &c.——*Quid enim est quod arte effici possit, nisi is, qui artem tractabit, multa perceperit?*] The Stoics derived all knowledge from experience. Now experience is a storing up in the memory of the distinguishing marks of objects by which we classify, recognise, and communicate our notions of them. But this group of marks is what we have termed the constant effect of a permanent cause—as by the general name *horse* we mean a certain bundle of qualities, or attributes, common to a great many objects which we therefore call by one name. The Stoics argued we should be disabled from acquiring any kind of knowledge if we were led to doubt the validity of the signs or marks by which we grouped external objects. Practically they were right, theoretically wrong, and principally they failed in pointing out any reliable method of induction by which the connection of an effect with its cause, or the sign with the thing of which it was a sign, could be verified. One can hardly imagine the Stoics themselves neglected such an important process of verification, although even theoretical. Scepticism is proof against the most overwhelming evidence. Sir G. C. Lewis would doubt, on seeing a man with a bullet in his heart, though otherwise completely intact, whether he was killed by this bullet (see Bain's *Logic*, Vol. II. p. 60). As we have so often stated, the signs or marks of things we call their qualities are effects, from the presence of which we infer their cause. But from the presence of an effect we can never infer a cause with theoretical certainty, unless we know *à priori* that no other cause could have produced the same effect. From the flower-beds being wet, we could not infer that it had rained in the night—they may have been watered, or there might have been dew. In the same way the marks or qualities of a horse may be present to my consciousness, but unless I can assert *à priori* that nothing else could have in any case produced these marks I cannot be sure that a horse is present—I may be dreaming—my nerves may be out of order, &c.

VIII. 23. *Ea autem constantia si nihil habeat percepti et cogniti, quæro unde nata sit aut quo modo?*] 'Since then our inward feelings and the perceptions we receive from our external senses are equally real, to argue from the former to life and conduct is as little liable to exception as to argue from the latter to absolute speculative truth.' (Butler, *Sermon* II.) The whole moral system of the Stoics was a rigid deduction from principles; but these principles were empirically induced from observation and experience of the laws of nature. Hence, if the faculties by which man acquired his knowledge were wanting in veracity, the whole art of life must fall to the ground, at least as a necessary, permanent, and natural standard of conduct, which the Stoics held it to be. The rules of life were, according to the Sceptics, founded on the laws of man. By the Dogmatists, on the laws of nature. By the one *man* was made the standard of good and evil, by the other *nature*. For example, justice with the Dogmatists would be the manifestation of the principle of harmony, order, and consistency, pervading all nature, while, with the Sceptics, it is but conformity to the arbitrary enactments of some individual or community. For an account of the ethical doctrine of the Stoics see *De Finibus*, Book III.; Diogenes Laertius, VII. 84; Stobæus, *Ecl. Eth.* p. 90 sqq.; Seneca, *Epistle* 89. 14.——*tam graves leges*] There is no better test of a man's belief than the amount he will endure for the sake of it.——24. *Ipsa vero sapientia......sapientiæ?*] The ultimate evidentness of some evidence is here appealed to. The final ground of wisdom or knowledge can no more be impugned than that of taste or relish, whence its name is derived—the crux of Greek speculation was, *how do you know, when you think you know, whether you know or not?* The English word *taste*, expressing the science of the beautiful, is sufficiently analogous to enable us to comprehend the point of view of the Ancients regarding knowledge. Nothing seems so subjective, artificial, conventional, and arbitrary as the judgments of men concerning the beautiful in art or nature, yet there is an objective standard—an ideal something, whither all opinions tend and converge. Philosophers have, in vain, endeavoured to resolve this into association, habit, custom; so with our moral judgments, towards which this part of the discussion evidently turns, *constitui necesse esse initium, quod sapientia, quum quid agere incipiat sequatur,* &c. It was supposed by the Peripatetics that the process of action in the case of an animal could be analysed into the following syllogistic form :

 1. Major Premiss. Such and such an action is universally good.
  Minor Premiss. This will be an action of the kind.
  Conclusion. Performance of the action.

See *De Motu Animalium,* VI. 2. Aristotle's *Eth.* Books VI. VII. *initium* = ἀρχή is the principle or major premiss, *idque esse naturæ accommodatum.* The standard of good and evil must be determined by nature, that is, nature as Bishop Butler understands it, viz. as decided by the cool, calm, dispassionate judgment of an intelligent being.——*appetitio* = ὁρμή. There is another form of the practical syllogism :

 2. Major Premiss. Such and such an end is desirable.
  Minor Premiss. This step will conduce to the end.
  Conclusion. Taking of the step.

With regard to these two forms Sir A. Grant observes (*Essay* IV. p. 214), "These two different ways of stating the practical syllogism are, in reality, coincident; for, assuming that all action is for some end, the major premiss may be said always to contain the statement of an end (*Eth.* VI. XII. 10). And again, any particular act which is the application of a moral principle may be said to be the means necessary to the realization of the principle. 'Temperance is good,' may be called either a general principle, or an expression of a desire for the habit of temperance. 'To abstain now will be temperate,' is an application of the principle, or again, it is the absolutely necessary means toward the attainment of the habit. For 'it is absurd, as Aristotle tells us' when one acts unjustly to talk of not wishing to be unjust, or when one acts intemperately of not wishing to be intemperate" (*Eth.* III. V. 13). We do not agree with Sir Alexander in his opinion that these two forms are coincident; in fact, neither does the first involve the second, nor the second imply the first. A man in concluding that such and such a course of action is good, does not necessarily desire it, and in desiring it he need not think about the good—at least this is a question lying at the bottom of all moral controversies. See *Gorgias*, 474 D. where Socrates is endeavouring to identify the base with the bad, i.e. the undesirable; and the right with the good or desirable——25. *Illud autem, quod movet prius oportet videri eique credi*] See Lecture II. § β, where we have attempted to explain how the Sceptics applied this principle.

VIII. 26. *si ista vera sunt*] The scholar will know that *ista* must be translated, the arguments of my opponents, i.e. the counter-arguments to the preceding reasoning.——*Quæstio autem est appetitio cognitionis quæstionisque finis inventio*] All desires are natural, i.e. have an end given and provided by nature. The Stoical argument will therefore be 'the desire of knowledge is natural,' 'the appropriate end is discovery or truth,' therefore truth is discoverable—in opposition to the Sceptics or Academicians who held truth to be ἀκατάληπτον.——*tum inventa dicuntur*] The word *invenio* does not convey the idea intended as well as our English 'discover' or German *entdecken*—*involuta* implies an analytic process which *invenio* does not.——*Sic et initium quaerendi et exitus percipiendi*, &c.] That which moves desire is also that which satisfies it, but that which moves the desire of knowledge is truth, therefore truth alone will satisfy it.

IX. 27. *quorum nullum sine scelere prodi poterit*] Cf. *De Fin.* III. v. 18, *A falsa autem assensione*, &c.] The Stoics held that to entertain a falsehood was a direct violation of the laws of nature, which were the standard of all virtue; for an objective fact, i.e. a reality, was among the Greeks the notion expressed by the term φύσει, and the antithesis of νόμῳ the mere subjective appearance. Thus the pursuit of truth was the highest virtue with the Stoics, for it was the coming face to face with nature and nature's laws. ——28. *Carneades acutius resistebat*] See ch. VI. 18 supra. *Qui enim negaret quidquam esse quod perciperetur*] *Self-evident evidence* we have before stated was the goal of Greek Philosophy. The question is, does the assertion there is no self-evident evidence assume a perception of this very fact—must there not be some light to make darkness visible? Carneades says 'No,' the Stoics 'Yes.' Whenever men disagree on first principles they are involved in the same difficulty. Carneades assumed *ignorance* as the natural condition of man, the Stoics *knowledge*. Then the Stoics called on Carneades to establish his position, while Carneades summoned the Stoics to prove theirs.——*decretum* = δόγμα, an empirical judgment, the very antithesis of ἐπιστήμη according to the Platonic doctrines, as our *à posteriori* knowledge is opposed to *à priori*.——*judicium veri et finem bonorum*] σοφία καὶ φρόνησις, theoretical and practical wisdom.——*cognoscendi initium*] First principles, such as axioms of geometry.——*extremum expetendi*] the objects of natural desire, which, being attained, are the natural causes of happiness, therefore the proper end of action for a wise man. The entire philosophy of the Stoics, with its aim, its method and its matter, is here compressed into a few lines.

X. 30. *Aliquantum a physicis*] Ch. VII. describes the process of acquiring knowledge. In this chapter *more* is intended but not executed; it is little else than a repetition of VII. For the distinction between ἐννοίας and προλήψεις see Lecture IV. ——*ipsa sensus est*] The Stoics allowed the mind the faculty of memory at any rate in addition to mere sensuous sensibility. Memory involves perception of self and time, neither of which ideas have their source in the senses, but are necessary to the exercise of sense, for unless the mind had been endowed with a retentive faculty the impressions of sense would no more leave a consciousness of themselves than the fleeting shadows of summer-clouds cause the lake in which they are pictured to be mindful of their presence.——*Cætera autem similitudinibus constituit*] The process of forming general notions as described in most text-books on Logic. See Thomson's *Laws of Thought*, ch. 2; Hamilton's *Lectures on Logic*. On perceiving that many objects are alike, we form them into groups or classes, and their points of resemblance constitute the key of recognition.——31. *quum ipsam per se amat......tum etiam propter usum*] Psychologists tell us that the senses have in the first instance a natural and spontaneous attraction to their objects, that infants are known instinctively to turn their eyes towards the window or fire, and are similarly fascinated by any intrusive sound if not so acute as to be painful to the membrane of the ear. Thus it seems the senses crave a sort of pabulum for their support and invigoration; and this appears to be implied in the text.—κατάληψις is the natural light of the understanding—self-evident evidence. Cicero translates it by *comprehensio*, but seems to warn his hearers it is merely for want of a better word in the unphilosophical Latin tongue.—— *quasi sensus alteros*] So by means of a balance we can discriminate differences of weight with more accuracy than by mere muscular sense.——*ut virtutem efficiat*] Knowledge of the laws of nature renders man able to obey them. Cf. *De Fin.* I. XIX. 63. Morati melius erimus, cum didicerimus quid natura desideret. ——32. *Quæ in profundo veritatem*] The school of extreme Sceptics is here dismissed as incurably illogical, inconsistent and impracticable. They were probably the Pyrrhonists and those of the New Academy who had adopted the views of the Pyrrhonists with theoretical rigour. Henceforth the doctrines to be considered are those of Carneades, who endeavoured to erect a standard of probability between the extremes of dogmatical certainty and sceptical doubt.——*Inter incertum et id, quod percipi non possit, &c.*] The mind is susceptible of degrees of belief according to the preponderance of testimony in one direction or another. So Carneades and the more rational of the New Academicians affirmed where demonstrative evidence was wanting there might still be sufficient to constitute a reasonable ground of probability. We shall see that the notion of the probable could not be theoretically supported, but Carneades was the first to maintain that probability was the only attainable rule of action. The difference between the unknown and the uncertain is not very precisely defined in this place.

XI. 33. *Si nihil interest,......notam*] To understand the Stoical argument let us suppose a traveller trusting to be guided to his destination by a beacon. If encountering an *ignis fatuus* he is unable to distinguish the illusive from the genuine mark. The real arbiter of his step would not be reason or evidence, but accident and chance. Such the Stoics thought would be the position of those who denied the self-evident character of evidence, *quidquam possit ita videri, ut non eodem modo falsum etiam possit videri.......sic reliqua visis*. The reader will remember that in Ch. VI., the cataleptic phantasm was rendered by *visum*.—— *probabilem et quæ non impediatur*] The probable judgment of Carneades was simply an inductive conclusion from the evidence of particulars as explained in Lect. V.——34. *perspicua a perceptis volunt distinguere*] I should conceive the distinction between *perspicua* and *percepta* to be the former referring to the *relation* of things, the latter to their nature. Of one we have ample and accessible evidence, of the other we know nothing. ——*Quo enim modo perspicue dixeris album esse aliquid*, &c.] Thus a black object is known relatively to a white with respect to its colour;—but of their absolute nature we can affirm nothing. From the Carneadean point of view a *black* object could not appear *white* because it would then be a *white* object. From the Stoical point of view, however, the colour would not be a mere relation of one object to another, but the determining objective quality, accident, mark or sign.——36. *notum iis esse debebit insigne veri*, &c.] Here we are round again at the same point, *how do we know when we think we know, whether we know or not?* Science with the ancients was a knowledge of causes, but the idea of cause was with them such that causes must for ever remain unperceived, because there was no faculty in man capable of apprehending them.

To an effect a multitude of causes may be assigned, and as long as they remain in the nebulous region of noumena it is impossible to apply the method of difference by which alone a real cause could be verified.

XII. 37. συγκατάθεσιν, see Lect. IV.——37—38. *Quae est in nostra sita potestate......perspicuam non approbare*] Assent = belief seems in one passage to be considered voluntary, in the other involuntary.

It is certain that determination to action depends solely on our belief in the reality of the existence of the object of desire. So far then as determination to action is voluntary the assent or belief is voluntary, but, regarding consciousness as a passive recipient of external impressions, it is involuntary. We speak about *weighing* an opinion, or *weighing* evidence, in which expression there is obviously a mixture of the voluntary and involuntary. We weigh the evidence, but the evidence influences us *ponderibus impositis*. Perhaps the meaning of συγκατάθεσις is not simply belief, but belief in external existence, as it is said belief = perception.——*Qui enim quid percipit, adsentitur statim*] Thus perception is used as in Reid's works, viz. the apprehension of the external *cause* of a change of consciousness. The measure of belief is the tendency to action. This was the cardinal maxim assumed by the Stoics.——39. *Omninoque ante videri*, &c.] See Lect. II. § β.

XIII. 40. The cause of the plaintiffs (the Stoics) is now closed, but their counsel Lucullus = Antiochus proceeds to set forth the counter-arguments of the defendants (the Sceptics = New Academicians), whose mouth-piece was Carneades represented in this work by Cicero himself.——*Componunt igitur primum artem quandam*, the science of succession and co-existence.——*Totidem verbis quot Stoici*] See Lect. V. § ϵ.

The theory of perception of the Stoics and Academicians was substantially the same. It was on the value and import of evidence that they were so irreconcilably opposed. The theory of perception is never explicitly set forth in this work, but is assumed as the basis of controversy by both sides. We have indicated it with sufficient detail in Lectures IV. and V.——*Quæ ita videantur......discerni non possint*] Compare with the four maxims given subsequently in this chapter, of which this passage is a condensation; but there appears something hopelessly obscure about it as here presented.——

41. Axiom 1. Quæ visa falsa sint, ea percipi non posse.
.... 2. Inter quæ..... alia ut non possint.
.... 3. Quæ videantur eorum alia vera esse, alia falsa.
.... 4. Omne visum... possit esse.

1. Mental images which are false cannot be perceived.

2. Of mental images among which there is no difference, it is impossible that some are of such a kind as to be perceived and others not.

3. Of things which appear, some are true, some are false.

4. Every mental image caused by a real object is of such a kind that it might have proceeded from an unreal one.

Compare XXVI. where, however, the order in which these axioms are stated is somewhat different:

        1 in XIII. corresponds with 2 in XXVI.
        2 .... 3 ....
        3 .... 1 ....
        4 ...... , ... 4 ....

The student had better consult XXVI. at once, the matter being identical though treated perhaps with more perspicuity.

We translate *visum* in every case here by mental image or representation, following the obvious meaning in Ch. VI. 18, reminding the reader, however, that the word image is only used figuratively, and that although *visum* seems to refer exclusively to the sense of sight, it is equally applicable to the representations of any other sense; there may be a *visum* of hearing, of taste, or of smell. We find no indication of the so-called *muscular sense* which plays so important a part in the doctrines of modern psychologists, and which has contributed more than any other to the elucidation of the subject of external perception. The question is, when are such mental images, being effects, signs, or marks of their causes, *valid evidence* of real external objects? By axiom 1, if the mark or sign is false, i.e. has not proceeded from the object, it is of course no evidence at all, i.e. cannot be perceived. The Stoics argued that this reality was a qualitative mark of the mental image, so that a man could distinguish between a dream and an objective fact. Carneades, on the other hand, maintained that there was no such qualitative distinction, that it was not the connection between the sign and the thing signified which influenced belief, but the relation of one sign to another; see Lect. V. § ε.——42. *Dividunt enim in partes*] This is the division observed in the δέκα τρόποι; see Lect. III. § β. A threefold relation, 1. Of object to organ of sense. 2. Object to object. 3. Object to the maxims of prejudice and tradition.

XIV. 43. *quod minime illi volunt*] An attempt is here made to refute the Academicians by showing that they would *invalidate* an *illative* argument by an *illative* process. But the Sceptics never questioned the illative process, as we have shown Lect. VI. § β. It is intuitive evidence they called in question.
——44. *Maxime autem convincuntur*, &c.] On holding a shell to the ear we fancy we perceive the distant murmur of the sea, but it is not the murmur of the sea; nevertheless it is not any qualitative difference in the mental image (*visum*) *qua* mental image, which assures us of the falsity of the representation, but a comparison of circumstances, such as the sea is 500 miles off, &c., besides the simple mode of verification by method of difference, i.e. by removing the shell—This is all the Academicians asserted.——
45. *Opinionem a perspicuitate*, &c.] Epicurus was what would now be called an *ultra-realist*—*materialist*, or an *intuitive realist*.

He considered that we envisaged material objects immediately, that when we said the sun of a foot diameter there was really an external sun of a foot diameter objectively presented; hence there was no inference, judgment or opinion, but a direct intuition, *perspicuitatas;* see note from Mill's *Logic,* Lect. IV. p. 73.

XV. 48. *Ut non modo non internoscat......omnino?*] The distinction between a false sensible impression and an erroneous judgment is here drawn between the thing distinguished and the faculty which distinguishes. With regard to the marks or sensuous modifications we have spoken above, Ch. XIII.——*Sin autem sunt,* &c.] Carneades and the New Academicians could not maintain the doctrine of probability consistently without admitting that the modifications of consciousness were reliable marks of external objects. Granting this, the Stoics maintained that it was as competent for a wise man to arrive at certainty as probability. But although this argument was available against the ultra-Sceptics, who founded on the equipoise of evidence, it missed the Carneadeans, who regarded probability as the *asymptote* to certainty always approaching, but never touching it.

XVI. 49. Soritas] See *infra* Ch. XXIX.——50. *Si quid cui......difficiliter possit?*] Two things may be similar in every respect but *one*—they are not therefore difficult to distinguish. And, even where marks are indiscernible, the objects are not identical—as several shillings are indistinguishable but not identical.——51. *Nam ab omnibus ejusdem modi visis,* &c.] This is exactly the reasoning advanced by Carneades; see Lect. V. § ϵ.

It is not any qualitative mark by which we recognize the reality of a mental mode, but simply by comparing it with juxta events. In respect to the illustrations from dreams, insanity, &c., it must be remarked that there is a wide difference between our judgments concerning dreams while dreaming and afterwards (XXVII. 88). In the first place, when dreaming we never question the reality of our perceptions; when we begin to do so it is a sure sign sleep is quitting us. When we dream that we dream it is near the awakening. In drunkenness or madness there is no doubt an overpowering intensity or heightening of the nervous state, which is a concomitant of the mental mode, while in dreams there is a corresponding enfeeblement. Thus in madness there is an irresistible determination to action; in dreams,

I think, we are never powerfully moved, there is a lazy contemplation of a panorama, without surprise at its anomalies, without much interest in its vicissitudes.

XVIII. 56. *rerum singulas proprietates esse*] See Lect. IV. If everything has a distinguishing mark then there is no danger of making a wrong inference from the possibility of a plurality of causes. On the other hand, as we have shewn above, if many external objects produce the same or an indistinguishable mental mode, there is no means of inferring, when such a mental mode is produced, which particular object has caused it. But the Stoics insist that each separate object has some distinguishing quality, appreciable at least to him who is sagacious and industrious enough to detect it; which, affecting a correspondingly distinguishable mode of consciousness, becomes a sign of its external cause. Cf. 57. *ii quum ovum*, &c.——58. *neque id est contra nos*] The *id* refers here to the proverb that one egg is like another; still, as was observed above, great similarity does not imply indiscernibility. The illustration of the hen and the egg is perhaps a travesty of the relation between cause and effect as understood by the ancients.——59. *necessario nata est ἐποχή*] The nature of ἐποχή has been sufficiently dwelt upon in Lect. VI. As we have already noticed above (XIV. 49), the doctrine of the ἐποχή is more illogical than that of probability; for if there is such a power of weighing evidence that exact equipollence is the result, there must be the ability to discern preponderance. Cicero seems not to have understood the real character of the ἐποχή, for he regards it apparently as an *à priori* determination to resist all evidence, and an obstinate refusal to entertain it; *whereas* it is manifest that the ἐποχή was the deliberate suspension of judgment *after*, not *before*, the witnesses on both sides had been heard. Arcesilas undoubtedly imported the Pyrrhonian form of scepticism into the Academy. See Lect. V.

XIX. 62. *Provide etiam ne uni tibi istam sententiam minime liceat defendere*] 'Beware lest you, in advocating the worthlessness of all authority, cause your own opinion to be regarded with scant respect.'

XX. 66. *Visa enim ista quum acriter...tamen*] Translate *visa*, appearances. When appearances are strong my belief is enforced in the reality of their objects, although I would not admit that such reality is manifest. I may believe where I cannot prove. *visis cedo*] I yield to appearances.——*cavere ne capiatur, ne fallatur videre*] The *former* implies 'fallacies of deduction,' or 'logical fallacies;' the *latter*, 'fallacies of induction,' or 'extra-logical.' Cf. Whately's *Logic*, Chap. On Fallacies; Mill's *Logic*, Book v.

XXI. 67. *Hanc conclusionem...secundum*] The argument may be regarded as a Destructive-Hypothetical (see Whately's *Logic*).

If A is B, C is D, but C is not D; therefore A is not B. Or, categorically, Fig. 2, AEE.

 Fig. 2. A. All who believe form opinions.
    E. But the wise man is not one who forms an opinion.
    E. Therefore the wise man is not one who believes.

Arcesilas, it is said, admitted the first and second premiss. The syllogism of Carneades would be

 A. All who believe or assent form opinions.
 E. The wise man sometimes believes.
 E. Therefore the wise man sometimes forms opinions.

Thus, admitting the major premiss, *All who believe form opinions*, both Arcesilas and Carneades could maintain their point. The Stoics and Antiochus therefore denied this proposition.——*si adsensurus esset, etiam opinaturum*] To opine or form an opinion is to admit a proposition without evidence, or to admit an appearance as a reality, or to admit the known as a mark or sign of the unknown without having any ground, or only an insufficient ground, for connecting one with the other. Perhaps an opinion is never without some foundation, either in the experience of him who holds it, or of others in whom he trusts. An inductive process is the only one by which the connection between a sign and the thing signified can be established; but the ancients seem to have had no method of verifying induction; they therefore either rushed into Dogmatism or lapsed into Scepticism. To say then that nothing could be perceived was equivalent to denying the possibility of establishing any general proposition, hence of performing any ratiocinative process whatever, not because the validity of the process itself was impugned, but because the major premiss was infirm.——68. *a me sumpsero et quod tu mihi das*, &c.] If the ability to form general propositions be denied, then those who believe in them must do so without sufficient evidence, i.e. such belief is mere opinion. The major premiss then of the above syllogism will have to be granted, viz.

'*All who believe or assent form opinions.*'

The minor premiss every one grants, viz.

'*That the wise man does not form opinions.*'

The conclusion, therefore, is inevitable. It is the establishment of this major premiss, '*All who believe form opinions,*' grounded on the inability of man to affirm general propositions, that Cicero undertakes.——*Nitamur igitur, nihil posse percipi: etenim de eo omnis est controversia*] The question whether all assent or believe *does* involve the assumption of a general proposition, is fully argued by Mr Mill, Book II. ch. 3, where the possibility is discussed of assenting that A, B, or C is mortal, without having first virtually admitted the proposition, '*All men are mortal.*' If we admit Mr Mill's reasoning the proposition, '*All who believe form opinions,*' would not demand attention, being obviously untrue; if, however, the necessity of affirming a *particular* through a *general* be insisted upon, then there must be granted the ability to form general propositions, or the impotence of man to assent positively to anything. The student will do well to consult Mr Sidgwick's lucid exposition on this topic. See *Contemporary Review*, July, 1871, Article 9, '*Verification of Beliefs.*'

XXII. 70. *hæc Academicorum est una sententia*] viz. the incompetency of man to positive and general affirmation, assent, or belief.——71. *quæ a te, Luculle, dicta sunt*] The real business of the book here begins. Cicero expounds perspicuously and earnestly the doctrines of the New Academy as developed and determined by Carneades and Philo. The salient points of their system have been sufficiently indicated in Lectures V. and VI.

XXIII. 72. *Anaxagoras nivem nigram dixit esse*] *Water is black, snow is water, therefore snow is black.* A flagrant fallacy, since there are two middle terms, snow is not water but frozen water. Sextus E. notices this sophism as an example of the discrepancy between the conclusions of reason and the perceptions of sense (Hyp. I. 13.)——*ostentationis aut quæstus*, &c.] A view of the Sophists, much questioned at the present day, and especially by Grote the historian.——73. *Quid loquar de Democrito?*] There is no doubt that Democritus *first* drew attention to the distinction between reality and appearance, by showing that many qualities of *bodies* could be only *modifications* of the percipient subject. Cicero's object seems to be, besides showing that the most renowned philosophers agree with him, to claim moderation in comparison with them.——74. *Furere tibi Empedocles...dicere.*——'*Scire se nihil se scire*'] A portentous exception; for to know one's ignorance is the highest knowledge, and as completely unattainable as any other knowledge (see post Acad. xii. 45). Arcesilas saw the scope of Socrates' assertion. The admission of it, however, was the distinctive feature of the Pyrrhonist doctrine which Arcesilas had adopted.

XXIV. 75. *Stilponem, Diodorum, Alexinum*] Representatives of the Megaric school; one of the three minor sects which sprung up immediately among the hearers of Socrates, viz.—the Cynics under Antisthenes,—Cyrenaics under Aristippus,—Megarics under Euclid.——77. *Quid ergo id esset*] The student who wishes thoroughly to understand the controversy respecting the theory of perception and the bearing this controversy has upon the whole subject of certainty, knowledge, belief, assent and comprehension, will find its cradle in this passage. What things can be perceived? Of what things have we intuitive evidence? i.e. evidence which itself requires no evidence to establish its evidentness. The Stoics answered this cataleptic phantasm or *visum;* for definition of which, cf. Lect. IV., and what has been said above.

XXV. 80. *Quasi quæratur quid sit non quid videatur*] The *fact* is, there is only *one* candle, the *appearance* that there are *two*. But the point is, what inference can be drawn from appearance with regard to fact; the appearance or mental image being accepted as a mark or sign of the reality. The Epicureans held that there was no *à priori* ground for discrediting the testimony of the senses. They must first be convicted of falsity before their evidence is doubted. The Sceptic then would point to the example just adduced, the Epicurean would reply that the error was in the inference not in the mark. But this could not be urged here, although it might be in the case of the broken oar; there the appearance was objectively correct, although the inference was erroneous; the mental image was a broken oar, so would have been its representation on a *camera obscura*. In the case of the candle, however, the organ itself distorted the presentation.——81. *Videsne navem illam ? Stare nobis videtur:*] In the phenomenon of motion is most clearly presented the problem discussed in this dialogue, and which is the foundation of all metaphysical enquiries, viz. the relation of appearance to reality—the means of discerning one from the other—and of inferring one from the other. For centuries it was supposed that the sun moved round the earth, and to every one the appearance (*visum*) is so. But the examination of other cases of motion shows that the appearance to us would be the same whether the sun moved round us or we round the sun.

This then is what is termed the *subjective* or *phenomenal* side; the *objective* or *actual* being the reality or fact of the sun moving in space round the earth, or the earth round the sun. Whether the sun moved round the earth as one fact, or the earth round the sun as another, the *visum* would be identical. Here then was a *visum*, mark, sign, or appearance originating in what was true of such a kind that there might be a similar one originating in what was false. It was only by observing the inconsistency of this inference, with other facts of the same kind, that Copernicus was led to the conclusion that the sun, not the earth, was the centre of the planetary system.

In this case, as Carneades would have insisted, there was no qualitative mark by which to discern the real from the apparent. It was only by comparison and estimation of evidence that a high degree of probability, or, as it is termed, a theory, has been arrived at.

XXVI. 83. 1. *esse aliquod visum falsum*] For example, the appearance of the candle mentioned in the preceding chapter. Epicurus, as there stated, did not admit this axiom.——2. *id percipi non posse*] From a false appearance a true inference, i.e. knowledge or matter-of-fact could not be deduced. If the mark or sign is not the mark or sign we imagine it to be, how can a thing of which it is a mark or sign be rightly conceived? The correct meaning of *percipere* is to draw a true inference, i.e. a correct statement of a matter of fact.——3. *Inter quæ visa nihil intersit, &c.*] Of course this is a self-evident axiom; things which appear the same cannot be distinguished. 4. *Nullum esse visum verum*, &c.] This axiom is the great *crux* of contention. Cf. Ch. XIII.

Axiom 1 corresponds with 3 in XIII.
   2 .... 1 ....
   3 .... 3 ....
   4 .... 4 ....

84. *Incidebat in ejus modi visum*, &c.] Here the mark is true, but the inference false.

 Such and such marks are those of my friend.
 This person has such marks.
 Therefore this person is my friend.

So in Hudibras:

 "His notions fitted things so well,
 That which was which he could not tell."

The error is in the major premiss which contains the general notion—bundle of marks, or characteristics of my friend. Through inaccuracy of observation this notion or group of marks may be either so few, so indistinctly imagined or retained in the memory, that they will fit, agree, or conform to many individuals. The process is carefully analysed in the Theætetus. Let us apply the *four* axioms to the example we gave in the preceding chapter of the heliocentric and geocentric hypotheses. Taking the 1st, the marks are true marks, the 2nd and 3rd will have no place, but the 4th conclusively demonstrates the untenability of the Stoical position.

 The apparent direction of a body is its real direction.
 This is its apparent direction.
 Therefore this is its real direction.

Here again the major premiss is erroneous, but this could never have been discovered without extrinsic observation, which involves another inference, viz. that the case we are considering is analogous to other cases of motion besides other judgments and comparisons.

 XXVII. 88. *tum, quum videbantur*, &c.] See Ch. XVII. 51.
 XXVIII. 91. *Dialecticam inventam esse dicitis*, &c.] The word Dialectic has 3 significations. It refers to the conversational, cross-examining, eliminating method of Socrates. With Plato it

seems to signify the process of discovering *objective* truth by the analysis of ideas. Lastly, it was used by the Stoics as synonymous with Logic as the science of reasoning, i.e. of the employment of the discursive faculty.——*Plus autem pollicebatur.*] Ancient Logic professed to be a real science, i.e. a means of discovering objective truth. The value of its pretensions is here most accurately estimated. Logic investigates the manner in which conceptions or ideas of the mind are related to one another. But the external facts upon which such conceptions are based are not amenable to the laws of thought, but the laws of nature. These laws of nature are the matter of which science is composed. The laws of thought which Logic examines concern only the forms in which this matter is moulded by the mind. We may, however, extend the province of Logic so as to make it investigate the general theory of evidence, and then taking the results of observation and experience as its material, it will be a real organon for the discovery of facts by establishing rules according to which the estimation and acquisition of evidence may be directed.

XXIX. 92. *Multa pauca, magna parva*] It must be observed that the *sorites* sophism is only applicable to subjective and arbitrary conceptions such as are here indicated. For example, there is no doubt whether a man is on this side of a boundary line or the other, though the barrier of separation may be indefinitely narrow; but in the case of such distinctions as few, many, broad or narrow, since the limits have no real objective existence they have no real defining power. Sir William Hamilton remarks, (*Lectures on Logic*, Lect. XXIII. p. 464,) that the sorites "attempts, from the impossibility of assigning the limit of a relative notion, to show by continued interrogation the impossibility of its determination at all. There are certain notions which are only conceived as relative—as proportional, and whose limits we cannot assign by the gradual addition or detraction of one determination. But there is no consequence in the proposition that, if a notion cannot be determined in this manner, it is incapable of all determination, and therefore absolutely inconceivable and null."—With regard to these observations of Sir W. Hamilton we think it is the arbitrariness and *subjectivity* not the *relativity* of a notion which renders the *sorites* applicable to it. A colour, for instance, is not a relative notion (at least not in the same *sense* as magnitude or degree), and yet the *sorites* might successively present all the shades between white and black, and so argue black was white. The student must notice that the argument termed Sorites by modern logicians has no analogy to that indicated here, but is a chain of reasoning of the form A is B, B is C, C is D, &c., therefore A is D. The mode of application of this kind of ratiocination, which is in fact the real type of all ratiocination, is admirably analysed and illustrated in Mr Mill's *Logic*, II. 5. The following is Sir W. Hamilton's historical review of this fallacy, "Sorites, though a word in not unfrequent employment by ancient authors, nowhere occurs in any other logical meaning than that of a particular kind of sophism of which the Stoic Chrysippus was reputed the inventor (Persius, *Sat*. VI. 80). Σωρὸς you know in Greek means a *heap* or *pile* of any aggregated substances, as sand, wheat, &c. and *sorites*, literally a *heaper*, was a name given to a certain captious argument, which obtained in Latin from Cicero the denomination of *acervalis* (*De Div*. II. 4). This sophism, as applied by Eubulides (who is even stated by Laertius to be the inventor of the sorites in general), took the name of φαλακρὸς, *calvus*, the bald. It was asked, was a man bald who had so many thousand hairs? you answer, No: the antagonist goes on diminishing and diminishing the number, till you either admit that he who was not bald with a certain number of hairs, becomes bald when that complement is diminished by a single hair; or you go on denying him to be bald, until his head be hypothetically denuded. Such was the quibble which obtained the name of *Sorites, acervalis, climax, gradatio*, &c. This, it is evident, has no real analogy with the form of reasoning now known in logic under the name of *Sorites*. But when was the name perverted to this, its secondary signification? Of this I am confident, that the change was not older than the fifteenth century. It occurs in none of the logicians previous to that period" (Lect. XIX. pp. 375, 6, 7). I cannot help thinking that the Differential method in Pure Mathematics had its origin in reasoning of this kind.——95. *ars ista*] The rules of Logic.

ἀξίωμα] For the history of this word see Hamilton's Reid, Note A, § 5.——*Si te mentiri, dicis idque verum dicis, mentiris*] The words *idque verum est* contain the key of the fallacy. In a *hypothetical syllogism* it is not upon the fact asserted by a proposition that the argument rests, but upon the consequence of one proposition from another. Thus, *If A is B, C is D*, but *A is B*, therefore, *C is D*. Such a conclusion would rest upon the *admission* of the assertion *A is B*, but not upon the fact of A being B. There is therefore no question of truth or falsehood in the argument, but only of *admission*. (See Whately's *Logic*, On Hypotheticals; also Hamilton's *Lectures on Logic*, Lect. XXIII. p. 466, On the Sophisma heterozeteseos.)

XXX. 98. *Sin vitiose, minam Diogenes reddet*] The allusion is to the story told by Aulus Gellius, LV. ch. 10, of Protagoras and Euathlus.

XXXI. 99. *Non comprehensa neque percepta...omnis vita tollatur*] The doctrine of probability as held by Carneades in no way resembles the theory of chance elaborated by modern mathematicians (see Lect. V. § ϵ). The probable judgment was based on observation, and is analogous to an inductive inference established by the method of agreement and the joint method of agreement and difference. In like manner Bishop Butler, in his *Analogy*, argues that a reasonable probability is a sufficient ground of action for a wise man.

XXXII. 103. *Academicis placere esse rerum...et cognitum possit esse*] The philosophers of the Academy held that there are differences between things of such a kind that some appear probable and others the contrary. But this is not equivalent to saying that some of these can be perceived and others cannot, because many things which are false are probable, but nothing false can be perceived and known.——*veri et certi notam*] The possibility of any qualitative mark of truth is denied by the Academicians; qualitative evidence, however, is admitted, so that any degree of probability may be attained, and this is considered sufficient ground of action. With regard to the ontological or substantial nature of things it would seem that the Stoics as well as the Academicians had renounced the pursuit, and were both in this respect Sceptics. It will be remembered that in the Theætetus the question was discussed whether *cognition* equalled *right recognition*. It was implied, though never demonstrated, that it involved something more. The Stoics, however, had entirely abandoned the metaphysical point of view, and, as we have indicated elsewhere, we imagine that the Academicians had preserved the Platonic doctrine, and were indirectly defending it in subverting the theory of recognition as advanced by the Stoics.

XXXIII. 105. *expedito, soluto, libero*] Cf. πιθανὰς...πιθανὰς καὶ διεξωδευμένας...πιθανὰς καὶ περιωδευμένας καὶ ἀπερισπάστους. Hyp. I. 33. 227. *tamen non possis...defendere*] Of all these diverse appearances you could not say which is the permanent constant and natural quality of the sea with respect to colour.

XXXVI. 116. *In tris igitur partes*, &c.] They, says Sextus E. (*Adversus Logicos*, VII. 3—17), who divide Philosophy into three parts are unanimous in distinguishing them as Logic, Ethic, and Physic. The Stoics compare Philosophy to a fruitful field, in which *Physic* resembles the tall trees, *Ethic* the fragrant fruit, *Logic* the strong wall. And others liken her to an egg; *Ethic* is the yolk, or embryo, *Physic* the white, or nourishment to the yolk, *Logic* the shell.

XXXVII. 118. *Princeps Thales*, &c.] With this catalogue of early Philosophers compare Aristotle, *Met.* I.——*Pythagorei ex numeris*, &c.] The Pythagoreans did not, as is vulgarly supposed, consider number the material cause of things. Number was with them the idea, form, or regulative principle, according to which the universe was constituted objectively, and construed by the mind subjectively. "νομικὰ γὰρ ἁ φύσις ἁ τῶ ἀριθμῶ καὶ ἀγεμονικὰ καὶ διδασκαλικὰ τῶ ἀπορουμένω παντὸς καὶ ἀγνοουμένω παντί, κ.τ.λ." (Stob. *Ecl.* p. 8.)——119. *eam sic animo*, &c.] That is, he will believe on evidence not demonstrative, for even the evidence of the senses is fallible with regard to objective existence. The presence of light is evidenced by a change of consciousness, but it would have to be proved that the objective fact of light could be the only cause of this change of consciousness before this evidence would be demonstrative. For a notice of the Stoical Pantheism see *De Nat. Deor.* Book II. Lect. V. § β.——120. *inter deos Myrmecides*] There must have been an idea of the Ant before its creation.——121. *Docet omnia effecta esse natura*] The student is recommended to read Cudworth's *Intellectual System*, Mosheim's Edition.

XXXIX. 122. *Nec eo tamen aiunt empirici*, &c.] Cf. Hyp. i. XXXIV. Note g.——123. *Hiretas Syracusius...moveretur*] In reference to this and the following chapters the student should consult Whewell's *History* and *Philosophy of the Inductive Sciences*.

NOTES ON THE LUCULLUS. 175

Platonem in Timaeo] See Jowett's *Dialogues of Plato;* Sir G. Lewis's *Astronomy of the Ancients;* Grote's Essay on the *Timæus*. Whether Plato understood the diurnal rotation of the earth or not seems to depend on the meaning we attach to the word εἰλλομένην, which may either signify "revolving," or compacted, as Mr Jowett calls it.

XL. 125. *aut inane*, &c.] This and the following are the theories of Democritus, adopted by Epicurus, and expounded in the poem of Lucretius, *De Rerum Naturâ*. See also Theophrastus, *De Sensu*, 63, Lect. III. p. 42.

XLII. 129. *Megaricorum fuit nobilis disciplina*, &c.] The minor sects, springing directly from the teaching of Socrates, are here enumerated. Cf. Lecture I. p. 10.——131. *Et vetus Academia*] See Appendix B. Madvig's Excursus IV.

XLV. 138. *prima naturæ*] See Appendix B. Madvig's Excursus IV. For a fuller account of the moral doctrines Cicero here sketches the student must consult the *De Finibus*.

XLVI. 142. *id cuique verum esse, quod cuique videatur*] This is a definition, not a proposition.

APPENDIX B.

EXCURSUS IV.

TRANSLATED from MADVIG's Edition of the *De Finibus* OF CICERO. On the Formula "Prima Naturæ," and the Carneadean division of the opinions concerning the 'Chief good.' *De Finibus*. Book II. chap. 11., Book V. chap. 6, and elsewhere.

1. CICERO in this work frequently introduces the formula 'prima naturae,' both by this particular name and by others differing slightly from it, but, as if the meaning were obvious and everywhere the same, he omits in any place to explain clearly and methodically the force of the expression or the nature of the thing. Not only to the attentive student, however, will certain obscurities and difficulties present themselves, but even Cicero himself appears, whilst he follows others incautiously, or adds somewhat of his own, to have comprehended this notion vaguely, and in places to have applied it unskilfully—and without explanation such passages cannot be adequately understood or criticised. Many writers on the history of philosophy have either entirely omitted or but cursorily treated this matter, because in the philosophical treatises of the Greeks the subject is rarely discussed, and in the annals of diverse sects it only attained prominence in those later writings Cicero followed. Beier, one of the commentators on Cicero (*De Off.* III. 13) has collected at random the various forms of expression Cicero uses without distinguishing their signification. Elsewhere, in his seventh Excursus on *De Off.* Book I., he has so commented as *there* not even to have alluded to the difficulty in question less patent perhaps in this work of Cicero; and in some places, while following his author, he appears to have discussed the form of this doctrine among ancient philosophers inaccurately. The difficulty

arises primarily from the fact that Carneades through his levity obscured a notion originally ill-defined by the Stoics among whom it arose; secondly, because Antiochus, on whom Cicero depends, imported it, with other Stoical theories, into the Academic and Peripatetic doctrines as reformed by himself; and the confusion is increased because Cicero, not content with a single and appropriate expression for *one and the same thing*, employs an unnecessary redundancy and variety of language, thereby confounding both in conception and expression those matters which even Antiochus had discriminated.

2. Τὰ πρῶτα κατὰ φύσιν (the equivalent Greek form for *prima naturæ*) is nowhere used by Aristotle, nor is this form of expression attributed to the leaders of the Old Academy by any author except Cicero. He following Antiochus assigns alike to Aristotle and Polemo definitions of the '*summum bonum*' of this kind, "honeste vivere, fruentem iis rebus, quas *primas* homini *natura* conciliet" (*Acad.* II. 131), or again, "virtute adhibita, frui *primis* a *natura* datis" (*De Fin.* II. 34; cf. IV. 15, where the word primorum is not added); again, "adipisci, quæ essent *prima natura* quæque ipsa per se expetenda, aut omnia aut maxima" (*Acad.* I. 22), and in the 4th and 5th books of this work (*De Fin.*) he always credits those authors (Aristotle and Polemo) both with an idea of the thing and the employment of the expression. But although Cicero (v. 55) introduces Piso declaring that he had traced to their cradle all the ancient philosophers, especially the Peripatetics, I do not remember any expression of this kind in those passages of Aristotle's works where he defines the notion of the good; for (*Magn. Moral.* II. 7) when he disputes concerning virtue, instituting a comparison between children and beasts, and investigates the laws of desire and aversion, he does not even use the contrasting forms τῶν κατὰ φύσιν or τῶν παρὰ φύσιν. The Stoics enquiring into the principles of action, estimation, and selection, argued that a certain primary appetition, *primus appetitus*, is apparent in every animal yearning towards that which nature herself had commended and made attractive to the creature. For thus Cicero renders what in Greek Chrysippus and others were wont to call οἰκειοῦν and οἰκείωσιν. They said that this attraction promoted self-regard, and the maintenance by the animal of its own condition or constitution. Hence, therefore, arose desire for those things conducive

to self-preservation sought for by nature, and repugnance to contrary things which nature rejected because injurious to that condition. Those objects which they supposed to be thus desired by a primary impulse were not only declared to be κατὰ φύσιν, and the opposites παρὰ φύσιν (Stob. *Ecl. Eth.* p. 134, 142, 250; Plut. *adv. Stoic.* 23, p. 1069 F., Clem. Alexandr. *Strom.* II. p. 179, Sylb.), but because they were the first to move the appetite they were called τὰ πρῶτα κατὰ φύσιν (Plut. *adv. Stoic.* 26, p. 1071 A.; Lucianum, *Vit. Auct.* 23; Gellium, XII., 5, 7; Stobæum, *Ecl. Eth.* pp. 144, 148); Stobæus also uses the form τὰ πρῶτα παρὰ φύσιν, and p. 136, he designates those things προηγούμενα κατὰ φύσιν, which he elsewhere terms πρῶτα. Varro in Latin, in his book on philosophy (*apud August. de Civ. Dei*, XIX. 1 et 2), had called them *primigenia* and *prima naturæ;* Cicero says that some natural objects are *secundum naturam*, and others *contra* (in many places, as III. 21 and 31, IV. 25, V. 72); again he terms them *naturalia* (III. 61), and more emphatically *prima naturalia* (II. 34), but most frequently with Varro, *prima naturæ* (III. 30, IV. 41, 43, V. 21, 45), also *prima secundum naturam* (V. 18, 19, 45); in Book III. 61, *prima naturæ secunda* and *contraria* are conjoined (cf. Stob. p. 148). But he uses other terms and significations, such as the following: *principia naturæ* (III. 22, 23), or *principia naturalia* (II. 35, III. 17), *initia naturæ* (II. 38, III. 22), *prima naturæ conciliationes* (in the plural number, III. 22); we find also *prima appetitio naturalis* (ὁρμή, IV. 25, 26) *ea, quae secundum naturam sunt, appetens* (IV. 32). The same things are said Academ. I. 22, *prima esse natura*, where the ablative case is used, meaning that they occupy the first place by natural appointment; but in II. 34 they are somewhat exceptionally called *prima a natura data*, which has no reference to the *actual* acquisition of the things, but simply means that they are originally proposed and suggested by nature for acquisition; thus they are termed, IV. 18, *principia a natura data*. Advancing from this form Cicero has more concisely written (II. 33) *prima data esse natura*, i.e. by the law of nature (cf. IV. 17), in the same meaning III. 17, *prima ascita esse natura*, i.e. approved and selected for acquisition.

3. But although the Stoics do not appear to have profoundly analysed this idea of natural attraction (*prima conciliatio*) so as to render evident what and how much it might comprise, they argued

that in the course of time a light of reason having suddenly arisen, which in the infant had not been kindled, and the uniformity and propriety of nature having been experienced, a certain will to agree with a nature arose in which was present both virtue and perfection of reason. This *will* they separated emphatically from natural attraction, and declared that the good sought after differed in kind from those objects primarily desired. Therefore although virtue is in the highest degree an accordance with nature (III. 21, 22 note to v. 34), nevertheless natural attraction not only does not contain any disposition towards virtue (for then virtue would be found in those natural objects of desire which corresponded to this attraction), but not even can the germs and beginnings of virtue be thought of in it, if the Stoics would be consistent with themselves. Natural objects are sought for as such, but he who strives after the beginnings of virtue, seeks virtue herself; hence virtue is at once separated. Natural objects of desire are by the Stoics comprehended in the class of things indifferent τῶν ἀδιαφόρων (Stob. pp. 142, 148), and προηγμένα (p. 148). Therefore when Carneades instituted the acquisition of these primary objects of desire as the *summum bonum* there is said to be no addition made of virtue in any place (as is explained in note to IV. 15); and in the doctrine of the Peripatetics those things termed *bona corporis et externa* are called by Cicero himself (II. 34, 38), by Cato (III. 30), and in Book v. 21, *prima naturæ*. It does not appear, however, to have been accurately defined by the Stoics what particular things were included in this expression of *primorum;* but the perception, strength, and health of the body and senses generally ranked first, as II. 34, v. 18; Stob. p. 144. Gellius includes under this term the pleasures only of the body, and the removal of physical pains. Cicero, II. 34, adds (*ingenii motum*) the things which in the system of the Peripatetics are called involuntary virtues; the same are reckoned by Stobæus, p. 60, amongst the *prima naturæ*, and possibly understood by the Stoics in their objects of primary appetition or simple preference, which they also called προηγμένα (Dio. L. VII. 107). Although Cicero (III. 17) places τὰς καταλήψεις amongst the *prima naturæ*, or so conjoins them that unless they are of the same class it would not appear why they are spoken of together, yet this ἡ κατάληψις seems to be so peculiar to ripe reason, as scarcely to hold this position amongst the *prima naturæ*. Because the Stoics were wont to look for the origin of notions in the perceptions of the senses, κατάληψις was readily combined with the perfection of the senses, as in Stobæus (p. 148), ὑγίεια καὶ αἴσθησις, λέγω δὲ τὴν κατάληψιν. I still more wonder that technical aptitudes (*artes*) are included by Cicero because they are totally adverse to the notion of primaries.

Furthermore, when Cicero (v. 18) would attribute to the mind certain first principles as the sparks and seeds of virtue, he incautiously intermixes matter from a source of which I shall presently speak.

Finally, the Stoics are to be commended because they did not admit of pleasure among those things craved after by the animal part of one's nature, but said that it was ἐπιγέννημα (aftergrowth), the subsequent affection of a creature feeling that it has attained the primary objects of desire (cf. note to III. 17). In their anxiety, however, to oppose Aristippus and Epicurus they scarcely allowed this secondary place to pleasure (εἰ ἄρα ἐστίν), nor did they show how such a lower kind of pleasure was consistent with the nobler emotion experienced by a man through the consciousness of co-operating by virtuous conduct *with* that higher nature of which he was a part; hence they confused the subject and left a loophole for error.

4. Somewhat different from this idea of the primary objects of desire, if carefully considered, is that first constitution or institution of nature which in Books IV. (15 sqq.) and V. (24 sqq.) is explained by the system of Antiochus. This system, regarding the nature of man as a whole, whilst including the body, attaches much more importance to the mind and to the perfection of reason in the mind, i.e. virtue (IV. 17, 41; V. 36, &c.), so that, although virtue may not be present at the first dawn of consciousness it nevertheless springs from that constitution, and is desired in the same manner as other objects which are contained in it, claiming for itself, however, a far higher degree of consideration. But because the desire of preserving the body is the most marked instinct in the early life of an animal, it was incumbent on Antiochus to explain this in his constitution and connect it with his definition of the chief good; he therefore appropriates from the Stoics the appellation of *prima naturæ*, and although they are

EXCURSUS IV.

goods of the body, they are at last joined by Antiochus to virtue (IV. 41, 43, 47). Therefore that which among the Stoics constitutes the idea of natural attraction is not mentioned in a very great portion of the constitution of Antiochus.

5. Cicero, following Antiochus, does not notice this discrepancy, and argues through the whole of the fourth book as if it were altogether the same thing, and in his exordium actually states as much (§ 15, "constitutio illa prima naturæ, a qua tu quoque ordiebare"), then he continues to say afterwards that the Stoics and the Ancients (i.e. Antiochus) set out from the same principles. Hence the same name by which in Book III. 22 and 23 he had indicated *prima naturæ* calling them *principia naturæ* in the Fourth Book, he applies (perhaps more conveniently and accurately) to that constitution of nature the notion of which he supposes Zeno to have derived from Polemo (42), and which he says must be modified by him if he wished to retain his own views of the *summum bonum* (34). To whom Zeno, if he had been present, would have answered so far rightly, that his idea of good was not derived from natural attraction. But in this Fourth Book, where Cicero follows Antiochus closely, he errs only in supposing that the Stoics attributed much more than they did to this notion of natural attraction. In the second Book, where Cicero refutes Epicurus in his own person, he lapses into still greater error. For, when endeavouring to avail himself of the Antiochian notion of original adaptation in order to convict Epicurus of inconsistency (inasmuch as he, Epicurus, had not arrived at a view of the *summum bonum* corresponding with that form of it which he had laid down), he imprudently substituted the narrow view of the primary objects of desire of the Stoics, together with their catalogue of them, instead of that general view of the constitution of man entertained by Antiochus, saying that the rest of the philosophers agreed with him, thereby falling into an inexplicable distortion. For after he (Cicero) said that in the opinion of Polemo and Aristotle the *prima* were the limbs, senses, disposition, perfection of the body, health, he adds that hence arose their doctrine that to live according to nature was the *summum bonum*, that is, to enjoy in a virtuous manner those objects of desire primarily indicated by nature, *virtute adhibita, frui primis a natura datis.* Whereas what can be more obvious

even to a casual observer than that the living according to nature could have been so defined that there need not have been the least reference, among these primary objects of desire, to that which is the chief point in his (Cicero's) explication of a life in conformity to nature (*adhibita virtute*), whether the primary objects were these or far different ones? Hence he joins Calipho and Diodorus to the ancients in the same commendation for consistency, and appears to point them out as having held the same primaries; certainly he does not mention others, and yet they differ in the idea of the *summum bonum*. I have already explained in a note that Cicero seems to have said something concerning the *prima* of Aristippus, Hieronymus, and the Stoics, which he may have erased; but, whether he did or not, it is difficult to imagine what relation he supposed there was between the *prima* of the Stoics and a chief good founded on virtue alone; and it is the more to be wondered at, that a confusion so great as this should have overtaken Cicero, because, in that very division of the opinions concerning the chief good made by Carneades which Cicero employs after Antiochus, there was left some distinction among these notions.

6. Carneades eulogized by Cicero for his remarkable proficiency in dialectic (III. 41), although he displayed sufficient skill in controverting the superficial doctrines of the Stoics concerning the theory of knowledge, was not possessed by any ardent desire of investigating the truth, and had such a dislike to the minute labour of discriminating the exact character of notions and opinions, that he affected to treat them with rhetorical levity and flippancy. Nevertheless he prepared the way for Antiochus, who subsequently deserting his sect, amalgamated the doctrines of the Peripatetics, Academicians and Stoics. Carneades then undertook an exhaustive enumeration of the opinions of dissentient philosophers concerning the chief good. This division, approved by Antiochus, Cicero explains in Book v. 16 and following chapters. For Carneades having laid down as a first principle that the art of life as well as other arts had some extrinsic end in view, and that such end ought to be consistent with, and adapted to nature, affirmed that the whole diversity of opinion was about primary appetition (*de primo appetitu*), and that on that point there were three doctrines; for some thought that pleasure was aimed

at by it; others, freedom from pain; others, all natural objects of desire. In this exposition it appears, firstly, that the primary appetition occupies such a place, that in it the entire bias of human nature is contained, and from it every good springs. So far therefore it corresponds with that primary constitution set forth by Antiochus. Cicero also (17 and 19) designates it by the term 'normal incitements,' *primorum invitamentorum*, and natural motives, *principiorum naturalium*. Further, it is manifest that this instinct is so defined as to be restricted entirely to self love and regard for the body, excluding all those things which subject a man to the law of reason and universal nature. From this point of view therefore this appetition or instinct resembles the natural attraction (*conciliatio*) of the Stoics, whence also Carneades derived the *prima naturæ*. Virtue is so far banished that those who would place her among natural goods find only a collateral admission. It is very extraordinary how Antiochus could have approved of this classification of Carneades, cancelling as it did its own conception of a primary constitution, in which the whole man and the perfection of reason are contained. The Stoics, indeed, were the last to allow that which Carneades laid down as a first principle, viz. that the art of life was determined by any extrinsic end, maintaining rather that it was wisdom entirely engrossed in itself (III. 24). Moreover, Carneades in his enumeration has most clumsily compared pleasure (i.e. as I have said the emotion of a man who has gained the object of his desire) with the *prima naturæ*, that is, with the very objects desired, and has placed exemption from pain (the negative idea of pleasure) as a distinct member of the division; an error which soon generates other obscurities.

Hence we have the following table of ends :

    A. To seek after

    1. Pleasure.
    2. Freedom from pain.
    3. Natural objects of desire.

    B. To do all things

    1. For the sake of pleasure,
    2. or exemption from pain,
    3. or natural objects of desire.

7. From these premisses, Carneades, although he appears to be intending to find *tria summa bona*, from the gratification of a threefold primary instinct, suddenly deduces an inference for which not the least ground or cause had been shewn, viz. that virtue is the doing all things for the sake of anyone of those three ends (see Table), whereof some said one was chiefly to be desired, and some another, even though a man might not gain the object of his desire. Consequently not only does he reach the idea of duty through that primary instinct, but, what is still more remarkable, although the notion of good had been evolved out of the gratification of a natural desire, we are all at once confronted with some who place the chief good in virtue *per se*, when even natural desire has not been satisfied at all. It is manifest that this remarkable method of reasoning originated from the definition Antipater of Tarsus was in the habit of employing, when he said that virtue or the chief good, is πᾶν τὸ καθ' αὑτὸν ποιεῖν πρὸς τὸ τυγχάνειν τῶν προηγουμένων κατὰ φύσιν (see III. 22); and which definition I am inclined to suspect had been already laid down by Diogenes (v. 20). This definition, while it attempts to associate with the notion of virtue one of duty rudely constructed from the selection of τῶν προηγουμένων, although it implies a contempt of *utility* for the sake of a higher law, greatly obscures the significance of virtue as understood by Zeno, and separates it from its true source, viz. the universal law of nature, to which it is voluntarily subject. From the rest of their system, however, it was apparent how virtue might be determined, and how it might contain good separated from the acquisition of *utilities*. Carneades both omits this portion of the doctrine, and contrives two other virtues, viz. pleasure and exemption from pain, opining that in these any one may find a happy life. We are not surprised then that those two doctrines concerning the chief good so ineptly devised should have found no defender.

8. Carneades also contended that, in addition to these simple notions concerning the chief good, there were three complex, made by combining the former in twos. The first that of the Academics and Peripatetics, the second that of Callipho, the third of Diodorus, and that there could not possibly be more if the nature of the subject were thoroughly examined. But if the original division of Carneades be correct, six compound notions should have been

EXCURSUS IV.

formed out of four simple ones (i.e. taking them two together); nor is it apparent why, if pleasure and freedom from pain were radically distinct both from each other and the *prima naturæ*, either pleasure and exemption from pain, or each of them and *prima naturæ*, may not have been properly combined.

9. Moreover, Carneades, who had originated this division, did not the less persistently oppose it, inasmuch as he maintained that there was no dispute about facts between the Stoics and Peripatetics (III. 41), of whom one held the simple, the other the complex notion concerning the chief good, which is equivalent to annulling that whole division and neutralizing whatever truth it contained. Antiochus, however, approved both of this division and of this opinion respecting the Peripatetics and Stoics.

EXCURSUS V.

On the arrangement of the Subject-matter in the Third Book of the *De Finibus*, and on the division of Ethic among the Stoics.

1. Although the Stoics themselves were wont to boast of the admirable arrangement and systematization of their doctrines, yet in every highly developed theory ideas are so linked together, that for their due consideration it is very necessary they should be set forth in regular order. We are therefore justified in enquiring whether Cicero in his exposition of the Stoical doctrines has followed the plan and sequence of matter adopted by this school itself; and this appears to be the more necessary because although we do not hesitate as to the general plan, we have expressed a doubt whether the arrangement of some few matters has been altogether satisfactorily executed; and even recently a learned man has attempted to discover some new principle of division of the Stoical Ethic, and to substantiate it from this very third book.

2. In the first place, since the system of the Stoics after the age of Zeno (their chief legislator and preceptor) had been amplified and developed by the exigencies of controversy, and certain notions not a little modified, it is evident that we might expect to find a considerable variation between the original form of their doctrine and that which generally obtained after the time of Chrysippus. But it is not certain that Chrysippus himself, although he seems to have included every part, preserved a systematic arrangement of the whole code, inasmuch as he treated of the leading subjects separately, and not in one continuous discourse. Nevertheless the very nature and affinity of the tenets of the Stoics, and their method of deducing and treating them as from one source, seem to have determined a certain sequence of the chief heads common to Chrysippus and those who succeeded him, especially since little care was taken to reduce ethic to first principles, or to connect it

EXCURSUS V.

at all closely or radically with theology and physic, *both* fruitful occasions of schism. Variety of order chiefly attaches to their treatment of individual virtues and actions. In Diogenes Laertius and Stobæus, as well as in Cicero, we have some indication of that sequence and arrangement of parts to which I am alluding, but, as might be anticipated in that class of writers, an indication not without obscurity. Diogenes (VII. 84) says, that ethic is divided by the Stoics εἰς τε τὸν περὶ ὁρμῆς καὶ εἰς τὸν περὶ ἀγαθῶν καὶ κακῶν τόπον καὶ εἰς τὸν περὶ παθῶν καὶ περὶ ἀρετῆς καὶ περὶ τέλους περί τε τῆς πρώτης ἀξίας καὶ τῶν πράξεων καὶ περὶ τῶν καθηκόντων προτροπῶν τε καὶ ἀποτροπῶν. It is evident at the first glance that in this enumeration cognate matters are disjoined, and the same things repeated as if they were different, because they had necessarily been discussed on separate occasions. For, how could the question of ends be dissociated from the discussion of good and evil?

And it is manifest from the brief notice of Cicero (§ 20) how very closely bound up with the question of intrinsic value (ἀξίας) is that concerning the primary appetition and natural attraction. These points were both touched upon as prefatory to the notion of the good, and subsequently more fully treated of when the distinction between things in relation to action and duty was discussed (§ 50). The same may be said concerning the notion of virtue which, divided from the good and evil, is interplaced between τὰ πάθη and τὸ τέλος. Nor are αἱ πράξεις and τὰ καθήκοντα properly disjoined. Moreover, what I now say is confirmed by the next paragraph (85) of Diogenes himself in the explanation of this doctrine, where, although roughly treated, the incongruities to which I have referred are for the most part avoided. For, from the normal appetition (85) he proceeds to the chief good (87), and to virtue (90), in which the chief good lies; then the notions and divisions of good are set forth (94), and the virtues in which the chief good is are indicated (100).

Then follows the technical distinction τῶν ἀδιαφόρων (of things neither virtuous nor vicious, 104); next duty is explained (107). To this exposition of things pertaining to a well-regulated life is added a notice of the passions (τῶν παθῶν, 110), with which are contrasted the lawful affections of the mind (ἡ χαρὰ τῇ ἡδονῇ). Annexed is a description of a wise man and in what he differs from a fool (116), which, while containing multifarious precepts for the conduct of life, somewhat inopportunely includes the maxim that all faults are equal (120). The doctrine of the identity of all virtue is added (125), as well as τῇ προκοπῇ (127), growth, the perpetuity of virtue, and its all-sufficiency for happiness, obviously belonging where the general nature of virtue was discussed. Still as these matters were frequently canvassed separately, and in the person and example of a wise man the characteristics of virtue and maxims for the conduct of life were set forth, I do not deny that Diogenes Laertius had some of the Stoics to countenance his arrangement.

A misplaced expression of opinion, defending the law of nature against the Epicureans, belongs to those precepts of life to which I have referred. If we carefully compare with this order of Diogenes Laertius that observed by Cicero, we shall easily see that although some things are differently arranged, and some found in one which are omitted in the other (indeed the design of Cicero's work altogether excluded those special precepts for the conduct of life), there is yet that similarity in the consecution of chief points which I have above indicated, arising from the nature of the ideas involved. For from primary appetition Cicero advances to the good, and the end, and to the nature of virtue, then to the distinction of things indifferent (τῶν ἀδιαφόρων), lastly, to duty by which the conduct of life is guided. Stobæus obscures to a much greater degree the continuity of the matters and opinions constituting the ethical system of the Stoics (*Ecl. Eth.* p. 90 sqq.), and dwells upon subjects of which I shall merely mention the names; good and evil (90); the definitions and divisions of the good (96); virtues (102); their end, the living according to nature (108); the identity of virtues (112); the character of the wise man (120); the division of goods (124); the end, to live consistently (132); τὰ ἀδιάφορα (142); duty (158); desire (ὁρμή, 160); passions (166); friendship (186); the character of a wise man, and general precepts (188); the definition of κατορθώματος and ἁμαρτήματος (192); equality of faults (198). It is plain that at the commencement the mention of appetite and natural attraction is omitted, whereas in the explanation of the end, and of the good, things intimately connected are separated and arranged apart. But here also, as with Cicero and Diogenes Laertius, duty is treated of immediately after τὰ ἀδιάφορα. Passions,

EXCURSUS V. 189

in explaining which the idea of appetition is involved, are treated of after duty, as with Diogenes.

3. Cicero, as I have already remarked, observes the same order as Diogenes Laertius. He has obscured it, however, either by his scholastic handling, or, as those who are well acquainted with this kind of Cicero's works will more probably think, he has derived it from that Greek writer whom he had elected as his guide when composing the book. And this is confirmed by the fact that Cicero himself in the person of Cato openly declares that the order of matter was suggested to him from elsewhere, 33, and especially 50. But this author, if a single one, was not Chrysippus, as Petersen thinks with Gorentz (Introduction, p. xxv.), although the discussion of Cato is deduced from a sentiment precisely analogous to that of Chrysippus in Diogenes Laertius, but was either Diogenes the Babylonian, or some one later than Diogenes who had made use of his work.

For, both that exposition of Chrysippus of natural attraction, and other subjects in this book attributable to him, as those which are mentioned §§ 27, 46, 61 and 73, together with those in which Cicero himself describes Chrysippus by name, 57 and 67, were communicated without doubt by him to others, as well as to his pupil Diogenes, whom Cicero himself in a former place joins to Chrysippus. But Cicero so follows Diogenes, even in a matter in which there was some divergence from the Stoics, that he seems to have chosen him as his authority (33), and he intrudes his opinion concerning the power of riches (49), too inopportunely for him to have done, unless he had had Diogenes' book in his hand, and had extracted copiously from it. And that part of the discussion, in which is expounded the difference of opinion between the Stoics and Peripatetics (41 sqq.), although it contains the maxims and opinions of all the Stoics, nevertheless seems to have been derived from some one else, who like Diogenes had lived contemporary with Carneades or after him. Nor is that to be overlooked, which is adverted to in § 22, that Cicero speaks of a formula of the *summum bonum*, attributed to Antipater a disciple of Diogenes, which would not be inconsistent with Diogenes himself. As to his indication of Stoics later than Diogenes (57), he might very easily have added sentiments about glory and fame from Panætius and Posidonius, with whose writings he was extremely familiar, notwithstanding that in the more profound reasoning of this whole book he had Diogenes or some follower of Diogenes as his guide.

But whether Cicero has followed Diogenes or any one else, or one or more in the composition of this book, it appears that whencesoever he derived his material, he found the subject already treated in the manner of the later Stoics, as if the aim was to determine and to corroborate the same notions in many different ways, sometimes following the pervading spirit of the whole system, sometimes contending with arguments deduced in conformity with some special doctrine, whence it easily happened that the same things were often repeated, and cohering doctrines were in some measure sundered. That something of this kind had happened in the part of this book where the good and the virtuous and the end are defined, we have already intimated (25 and 34), and still more might be remarked. For, 26, 27, by a new mode of argumentation nothing is accomplished but what had been already demonstrated, and after it is here explained that virtue is the only good (36), it is reiterated that virtue must be sought for its own sake. Cicero, again, when extensively extracting the main heads of opinions from one or more Greek writers relating to the chief good and quality of things, seems in two places (35, 49) to have inadvertently retained something which may originally have been connected with another discussion, and to have placed it in his book, so that it does not appear to what it refers, or what it has to do with the matter. Finally, in the midst of the exposition τῶν ἀδιαφόρων (55), he suddenly introduces a division of goods, as if it belonged there, *sequitur illa divisio ut bonorum alia sint,* &c., which it is evident ought to have been placed where he was speaking of the conception and definition of the good, as is the case in Stobaeus (p. 100) and Diogenes Laertius (VII. 96, sqq.). Either Cicero introduced it here, thinking of a similar enumeration τῶν προηγμένων affixed to § 56, or because in the Greek writer whom he followed he found it in this connection for the sake of comparison.

www.ingramcontent.com/pod-product-compliance
Lightning Source LLC
Chambersburg PA
CBHW032137160426
43197CB00008B/681